The Moral and Political
Philosophy of Immigration

The Moral and Political Philosophy of Immigration

Liberty, Security, and Equality

José Jorge Mendoza

LEXINGTON BOOKS
Lanham • Boulder • New York • London

Published by Lexington Books
An imprint of The Rowman & Littlefield Publishing Group, Inc.
4501 Forbes Boulevard, Suite 200, Lanham, Maryland 20706
www.rowman.com

Unit A, Whitacre Mews, 26-34 Stannary Street, London SE11 4AB

British Library Cataloguing in Publication Information Available

Library of Congress Cataloging-in-Publication Data Available

ISBN 978-1-4985-0851-3 (cloth : alk. paper)
ISBN 978-1-4985-0853-7 (pbk. : alk. paper)
ISBN 978-1-4985-0852-0 (Electronic)

∞™ The paper used in this publication meets the minimum requirements of American National Standard for Information Sciences—Permanence of Paper for Printed Library Materials, ANSI/NISO Z39.48-1992.

Printed in the United States of America

Para mis padres, Lupe y José, con mucho amor.

Contents

Acknowledgments

This book would not have been possible without the help and support of countless people. Beginning with my family, I would like to thank my mother Guadalupe Marin, my father José Mendoza, my sister Lorena Mendoza, my brother Nino G. Mendoza, my nieces and nephews Jonathon, Juliana, Logan, and Shanti, my parents-in-law Sheryl and Peter Wirts, and also my "brothers from another mother" Enrique Perez, Octavio Perez, Carlos Rico (RIP), Israel Rivera, Leo Sandoval, James Taylor, Scott "Woody" Wood, Omar Zuniga and all of their families who have treated me always as one of their own. Most especially I would like to thank my life partner, Amelia Wirts, who never tired of discussing all of the ideas in this book with me, read various drafts of the chapters, and provided invaluable feedback and emotional support during the entire process.

I would also like to thank all of my mentors who played key roles at various critical junctures in my life and career. Without them I would not be where I am today and this book would not have been possible. The most sincerest of thank yous to Anatole Anton, Kostas "Gus" Bagakis, Edward Olivos, Roberto Rivera, Cheyney Ryan and Naomi Zack. I hope that you see a little bit of your influence reflected back to you in this book.

Lastly I would like to thank all of my friends and colleagues for their support throughout the years: Brandon Absher, Linda Alcoff, Stephanie Rivera Berruz, Michael Blake, Larry Blum, Danielle Bromwich, Michael Philip Brown, Paul Bucher, Elizabeth Caldwell, Joseph Carens, Justin Akers Chacón, Aviva Chomsky, Tommie Curry, Adrian Cruz, Kim Diaz, Enrique Dussel, Elena Cuffari, Richard Daniels, Nick Evans, George Fourlas, Al Frankoski, Heidi Furey, Jazmine Lily Gabriel, Jorge L. A. Garcia, Francisco Gallegos, Lori Gallegos, Jorge J. E. Gracia. Aldo Guevara, Sally Haslanger, Carol Hay, Peter Higgins, Christa Hodapp, Adam Hosein, Emma Jones,

David Anton Johnson, Jason Jordan, John Kaag, Whitley Kaufman, David Kim, Chandran Kukathas, Sarah LaChance-Adams, David Leech, Matt Lister, Federica Liveriero, Johanna Luttrell, John Lysaker, James Maffie, Mauricio Magaña, Phil Mayo, Howard McGary, Lionel McPherson, Jennifer McWeeny, Eduardo Mendieta, Charles Mills, Elizabeth Millán, Todd Miller, Megan Mitchell, Michael Monahan, Amy Oliver, Luis Oliveira, José-Antonio Orosco, Mariana Ortega, Cynthia Paccacerqua, Gregory Pappas, Serena Parekh, Mickaella Perina, Geoffrey Pfeifer, Andrea Pitts, Scott Pratt, Sandra Raponi, David Rasmussen, Amy Reed-Sandoval, Joel Michael Reynolds, Nick Reynolds, Lisa Rivera, Dana Rognilie, Alex Sager, Carlos Sanchez, Robert Eli Sanchez, Alejandro Santana, Richard Schmitt, Ofelia Schutte, Daniel Shartin, Tommy Shelby, Falguni Sheth, Grant Silva, Andrew Soto, Ronald Sundstrom, Edgar Temam, Henry Theriault, Alejandro Vallega, Daniela Vallega-Neu, Manuel Vargas, Ernesto Rosen Velasquez, Kristin Waters, Shelley Wilcox, and Rocío Zambrana.

Introduction

Philosophy and the Issue of Immigration

Recently, moral and political philosophers have taken an interest in the issue of immigration. This newfound interest might seem curious to some, especially considering that most of the important questions surrounding immigration appear to be empirical in nature and thereby more within the purview of disciplines in the social sciences than in the humanities. Furthermore, the study of immigration is not a task that is typically done for its own sake, but usually done with the aim of helping to shape or influence real world public policy. Many (including some philosophers) would consider this sort of task to be antithetical to the study of philosophy. It is therefore not surprising that some might be sceptical about the meaningful contribution philosophy has to make toward the development of a real world immigration policy.

This book attempts to answer this challenge by arguing that the immigration debate is primarily a conflict over competing moral and political principles. In other words, the more significant disputes that arise within immigration debates are not so much about conflicting empirical facts, but about competing moral and political commitments. This is not to say that empirical research is inconsequential to the immigration debate, but to say that the meaningfulness of such research always requires interpretation and this is where much of the normative action is at. So while it is true that resolving disagreements over evidence (i.e., over matters of fact) might best be left to social scientists, understanding and addressing disagreements over values and norms (i.e., what these facts *ought* to mean or what *ought* to be done in light of them) is an area where philosophers are uniquely qualified to make important contributions.

Philosophy, however, has only recently begun taking up the issue of immigration and has done so largely by treating it as one among many topics in "applied ethics." Philosophers have approached the issue of immigration this way in part because of a growing trend of treating philosophy as though it were merely a handmaiden to the sciences. This book emphatically rejects this treatment of philosophy. Instead, this book attempts to situate the issue of immigration at the heart of current Western moral and political philosophy, as an essential part of the story that tells about the nature of liberty, security, and equality. In other words, immigration is not simply a new riddle on which philosophers try out their competing conceptions of justice. Immigration is an important issue to consider because it exposes the limits of our current conceptions of justice and in doing so challenges us to rethink them. For this reason, the issue of immigration might be the most pressing issue that moral and political philosophers have to grapple with today.

Outline of the Argument

The immigration policy of most nation-states today is trapped in what I call a "security dilemma." This dilemma begins with the belief that unrestrained immigration (i.e., open-borders) presents a serious threat to security, which can take various forms, but is usually expressed in one of three ways: (1) unrestrained immigration poses a threat to the current form of government (e.g., immigrants undermine constitutional democracy); (2) unrestrained immigration is a threat to social welfare (e.g., immigration undermines social trust and social safety nets); (3) unrestrained immigration poses a threat to individuals (e.g., immigrants bring with them infectious diseases or proliferate crime).[1]

This belief is then coupled with a second belief, which is that the only way to effectively respond to the aforementioned threats is to give a regime (e.g., the US federal government) complete discretionary control over. The difficulty this then poses is that the proposed cure might turn out to be worse than the initial disease. A regime with complete discretionary power might be able to keep its citizens safe from certain external threats, but internally a regime with so much unrestrained power can itself become a major threat to its citizens. In short, when it comes to the issue of immigration, public policy makers are currently stuck trying to prevent a descent into what we might call a Hobbesian "state of nature," but their proposed solution only gives rise to what we might call an Agambenian "state of exception."

The solution I propose is that the *security dilemma* can be avoided altogether if principles of constitutional democracy were to be given priority. My overall argument in support of this claim has two parts. First, I argue that a concern for liberty ought to take precedence over a concern for security. Second, I argue that in privileging liberty over security the possibility of a stable and well-ordered political community is not foreclosed. The implication that a view like mine has for immigration is that all persons, including undocumented immigrants, ought to be entitled to certain basic protections from a regime's enforcement mechanism and that these protections will generate certain rights of entry that any legitimate political regime is bound to respect. Therefore, if my argument is successful it will show that it is not only possible for immigrants to have rights in a stable and well-ordered society, but that a stable and well-ordered society is premised on limiting the discretion a regime is normally thought to have over immigration. I call this view the minimalist defence of immigrant rights.

In order to arrive at this conclusion, however, more needs to be said about the nature of the *security dilemma* and how I propose to resolve it by giving priority to liberty over security. To do this, I begin in Chapter 1 by defending the following claim: prioritizing a concern for security over a concern for liberty is self-defeating. To make this case, I use the concrete example of the Plenary Power Doctrine, which is currently in effect today in the United States. This doctrine, which is grounded in US case law, allows the US federal government to regulate immigration free of judicial review and thereby, with respect to immigration, disregard many important constitutional protections that should be afforded to all persons. The normative reasoning behind this doctrine rests on the belief that limiting sovereign authority in matters of immigration would undermine its legitimacy and thereby lead to something like a Hobbesian state of nature.

In granting the federal government such broad and discretionary power over immigration, the courts have in turn risked placing both citizens and noncitizens in a situation that the Italian philosopher Giorgio Agamben has referred to as a state of exception. This therefore leaves us with the following dilemma: either we accept something like the Plenary Power Doctrine and risk ending up in Agambenian state of exception, or we reject this doctrine and risk descending into something like a Hobbesian state of nature. I argue that the way out of this dilemma is not to choose one prong or the other, but to instead begin again by giving priority to the liberty concern over the security concern. We must favour a form of sovereignty that gives priority to liberty and equality (e.g., a constitutional democracy) instead of one that leads to authoritarianism.

In doing so, we will find that all persons, including undocumented immigrants, are entitled to more protections than they are usually thought to enjoy. Furthermore, since extending these protections is more inline with a kind of sovereignty that is based on a system of checks-and-balances and respect for the basic liberties of individuals, curtailing the regime's control over immigration does not so much undermine, as it is consistent with, a stable and well-ordered society. Chapter 1 therefore concludes with the claim that giving priority to the liberty concern over the security concern will ameliorate, if not completely assuage, the more pernicious aspects of the *security dilemma* and it will do so without undermining the sovereignty of a political community.

In Chapter 2, I trace out the history of the liberty concern within modern moral and political philosophy. This outline is meant to show how, just as with the security concern, the liberty concern is made up of various con-flicting elements. Addressing the liberty concern requires a commitment to democratic self-determination, individual freedom and universal equality, but these three commitments do not always cohere well together. The tension between them is what I call the "liberty dilemma." The *liberty dilemma* is most clearly articulated in the contrast between classical liberalism and civic republicanism. On the one hand, classical liberalism gives priority to individual freedom, but does so at the expense of universal equality and democratic self-determination; while on the other hand, civic-republicanism prioritizes democratic self-determination and universal equality, but does so at the expense of individual freedom. The *liberty dilemma* therefore comes about from two competing notions of liberty: negative and positive liberty. Both notions of liberty are essential to constitutional democracy, but they are not easily made compatible. This therefore poses a problem for the conclusion I tried to advance at the end of Chapter 1. If the *security dilemma* can only be adequately resolved by appealing to a concept of sovereignty that gives priority to liberty, what happens if no such concept is possible due of the irresolvable tension between positive and negative notions of liberty?

Chapter 2 then takes a slight detour into the work of David Hume, who offers a powerful objection to the possibility of addressing the security concern in the manner I proposed in Chapter 1, by giving priority to the liberty concern over the security concern. Hume's objection leaves us with the following problem: if these two conflicting notions of liberty cannot be reconciled, then prioritizing the liberty concern over the security concern will offer little hope for establishing a stable and well-ordered society. If Hume is correct, then a stable and well-ordered society might only be possible by cultivating the right customs and habits. Ultimately, Hume's conservative objection will not be satisfactorily discharged until the end of Chapter 5, but part of the initial response to Hume is to suggest that the Kantian notion of autonomy can resolve the *liberty dilemma*, but only if it can also address strong objections raised by the utilitarian and Marxist traditions. In this regard, John Rawls's two principles of justice help supplement Kant's notion of autonomy by addressing these objections.

The problem with Rawls's account however is that it resolves the *liberty dilemma* only by assuming that political communities are already bounded, such that citizens enter only by birth and exit only in death. This assumption is important for the kind of buy-in that Rawls's theory of justice demands, but it is an assumption that is not feasible when the kind of justice we are looking for is more global or international in scope, like immigration justice. Without the assumption of a bounded society, the *liberty dilemma* returns in a new form: either too much freedom of movement can prove disruptive in obtaining a stable and well-ordered society or in order to justify the self-determination of democratic political communities we are forced to assume deep inequalities between citizens and noncitizens.

Chapter 3 provides an overview of this early philosophical debate over immigration. This overview is primarily focused on showing how the *liberty dilemma* has played out in this debate and how philosophers have favoured either one prong or the other of this dilemma. This chapter begins by presenting the communitarian position, which argues (contra Rawls) that questions of justice must begin by determining the boundaries of membership. On this view, a political community's existence is heavily dependent on having clear boundaries and because of this need to keep boundaries clear, political communities are presumptively entitled to control immigration.

This chapter then proceeds to a more traditionally liberal position, which argues that commitments to either individual freedom or universal equality entail that the borders between political communities must be as open as possible. In justifying this view, Joseph Carens outlines three traditionally liberal positions—the libertarianism of Robert Nozick, the egalitarianism of John Rawls, and utilitarianism broadly construed—and shows that when these three traditionally liberal positions are globalized, they can justify few (if any) restrictions on migration.

These two opposing views on immigration, then give rise to a third alternative, the liberal-nationalist position, which holds that maintaining commitments to individual freedom and universal equality is dependent on nation-states being able to control their own boundaries. Subsequently, the liberal-nationalist position is challenged on non-ideal grounds by the liberal cosmopolitan view. This view puts into question the liberal-nationalist assertion that the nation-state, as opposed to other political communities, should have the presumptive right to control immigration. They make the case that regardless of a nation-state's preference, some noncitizens have restorative justice claims that entitle them to admission or that membership in a transnational community grants certain noncitizens a right to admission.

In Chapter 4, I then look at Christopher Heath Wellman's innovative argument that appears to finally provide a resolution to the *liberty dilemma* as it has played out in the immigration debate. Wellman argues, from a traditionally liberal point of view, that a legitimate state (i.e., a state that respects human rights) is entitled to self-determination and that part of the definition of being self-determined includes "freedom of association." According to Wellman, freedom of association also entails a right not to associate, which for legitimate states means having a presumptive right to exclude noncitizens. This chapter concludes by looking at some of the criticisms that have already been levelled against Wellman's account. Each of these criticisms raises an important objection, but Wellman appears to have a ready reply for each and none of them in turn seem to offer any better way of getting the immigration debate out of the *liberty dilemma*.

In Chapter 5, I therefore put forth what I believe is a novel objection to Wellman's account, but one that also challenges the overall framing of the immigration debate within philosophy. My view is that moral and political philosophers have focused too much on questions of admission and exclusion and not enough on enforcement. On my view, concerns about how and to what extent immigrants can be coercively denied entry or removed overdetermine how much discretion a legitimate state ought to have over immigration. I make a case for this view by looking at how Wellman's proposed resolution to the *liberty dilemma* would account for the potential injustices of enforcement. My own view is that Wellman's resolution would not hold up. Instead, we would find that with respect to immigration enforcement a legitimate state's ability to control immigration should be checked at the border by a concern for the moral equality of noncitizens and internally by a concern for the political equality of citizens. These checks provide an indirect argument for why a legitimate state's right to control immigration should be circumscribed, not discretionary. In other words, we will see why the burden of proof ought to be on legitimate states to justify any immigration restrictions and not on immigrants to defend their movement across international boundaries. I call this view a minimalist defence of immigrant rights.

I then conclude the book by defending this view against two possible criticisms, the conservative and radical objections, and by showing what policy implications a view like mine would have for future immigration reform. I suggest a three-part framework that takes into account the past, present, and future implications of immigration reform. Since this starts to go beyond the scope of the book, the framework I provide is only a sketch. It is sufficient, however, to show (i) how the ethics of immigration can provide some normative guidance to real world public policy; (ii) why a minimalist defence of immigrant rights provides a better philosophical solution to both the *security* and *liberty dilemmas* than an approach like Wellman's; and (iii) why a minimalist defence of immigrant rights provides a better policy solution to the current "immigration problem" than any of the other policy reforms currently under discussion.

NOTE

1. Different versions of these arguments can be found in Samuel Huntington, *Who Are We? The Challenges to America's National Identity* (New York: Simon & Schuster Paperbacks, 2004); Peter Brimelow, *Alien Nation: Common Sense About America's Immigration Disaster* (New York: Harper Perennial, 1996); and Ann Coulter, *Adios, America: The Left's Plan to Turn Our Country into a Third World Hellhole* (Washington, DC: Regnery Publishing, 2015).

Chapter 1

The Security Concern and the Security Dilemma

In order to properly begin a philosophical discussion on the issue of immigration it is important to begin with two concerns that, at least since the modern period, have dominated Western moral and political thought. The first is the security concern, which stresses the importance of a political regime being able to keep its subjects safe and provide them with a stable and well-ordered society. The second is the liberty concern, which stresses the importance of a political regime being democratically self-determined and respectful of both individual freedom and universal equality. This chapter focuses on the former, the security concern, and an internal tension, which I have dubbed the "security dilemma," that arises when the security concern is given priority over the liberty concern.

The reason for beginning with the security concern, as opposed to the liberty concern, is that much of the politics of immigration today is stuck in a *security dilemma.* This dilemma arises when, for the sake of maintaining a stable and well-ordered society, a regime is given complete discretionary control over a particular area of governance. When this happens it is not unusual for the regime itself to become a threat to its subjects. In other words, a *security dilemma* arises when a proposed resolution to a security concern is self-defeating. In this chapter, I use the US Plenary Power Doctrine as an example of a *security dilemma.* The Plenary Power Doctrine, which the US federal government has operated under since the second half of the nineteenth century, gives the federal government complete discretionary control over immigration and thereby denies many essential constitutional protections to noncitizens in matters concerning their admission, exclusion, and removal. The justification for this broad and unchecked power is not technically one of the federal government's constitutionally enumerated powers,[1] but is the product of various nineteenth-century Supreme Court

1

decisions. In these cases, the Supreme Court determined that the power to
regulate immigration, meaning the power to admit, exclude, and remove noncitizens, is a chief attribute of sovereignty and therefore lies outside the scope
of judicial review.

This understanding of sovereignty assumes, at least with respect to matters such as immigration, that any limitation on a regime's power would
undermine its legitimacy and potentially place it in something like a Hobbesian "state of nature." While the risk of falling into a Hobbesian *state of
nature* should not be taken lightly, there is an equally hazardous downside
to granting any regime (in this case the US federal government) such broad
and unchecked discretion over matters like immigration. This downside is
best articulated in Giorgio Agamben's warning against the "state of exception." The *state of exception* is a situation in which the unrestrained power
of the sovereign, which is necessary to ward off a lawless and chaotic *state
of nature*, actually undermines rather than protects the safety of individuals.
With regard to immigration, this all-or-nothing view of sovereignty leads to
the following *security dilemma*: without something like the Plenary Power
Doctrine the US federal government risks falling into a *state of nature*, but the
kind of discretionary power that the Plenary Power Doctrine gives to the US
federal government is also what makes a *state of exception* possible.

This chapter therefore provides a two-part response to the *security
dilemma*. First, it argues that something like the Plenary Power Doctrine
is incompatible with the type of sovereignty embodied in constitutional
democracies. The legitimacy of constitutional democracies depends on
them providing certain protections to all individuals, including undocumented immigrants, and these protections undermine the kind of discretion
regimes are normally thought to enjoy over immigration. In this way, constitutional democracies are able to ward off a *state of exception*. Second,
since extending these protections, even to undocumented immigrants, is
 more consistent with the type of sovereignty expressed in a constitutional
democracy, curtailing the authority a regime has over immigration will not
only *not* lead to a *state of nature*, but will actually better promote its sovereignty. In short, the *security dilemma* that appears to arise with the issue
of immigration—which asks a regime to choose between either a *state of
nature* or a *state of exception*—is ultimately a false dichotomy when the
regime in question is a constitutional democracy.

PLENARY POWER DOCTRINE

In the US, the Plenary Power Doctrine is the culmination of various US
Supreme Court cases that have given the federal government complete

discretionary control over the admission, exclusion, and removal of noncitizens. The first set of Plenary Power cases are collectively known as the "1849 Passenger Cases." In these cases, the question before the court was whether it was constitutional for individual states to assess taxes on foreigners who disembarked on their ports. The court found that these state level taxes were unconstitutional because they violated the Commerce Clause of the Constitution.[2] The Commerce Clause grants the federal government, as opposed to local and state governments, the exclusive power to regulate interstate commerce as well as commerce with foreign nations. But while the central issues in the *Passenger Cases* were about taxation and commerce, the Court's decision ultimately had implications for immigration as well. These cases established the first component of the Plenary Power Doctrine: the federal government (and not state or local governments) has complete discretionary control over the admission of noncitizens.

The other two components of the Plenary Power Doctrine—the power to exclude and the power to remove noncitizens—were addressed in what have come to be known as the "Chinese Exclusion Cases." The first of these cases was the 1889 *Chae Chan Ping v. United States* case. In that case, the Supreme Court upheld the constitutionality of the 1882 Chinese Exclusion Act. This Act prohibited any further immigration from China and subsequently made all Chinese immigrants ineligible for US citizenship, thereby converting all Chinese nationals who were already present in the US into legal permanent residents (LPRs).[3]

The plaintiff in this case, Chae Chan Ping, was a Chinese LPR who went to China for a visit in 1887. At the time of his departure, Ping would have been allowed to return to the US through a policy, which was a part of the original Chinese Exclusion Act, of giving return vouchers to LPRs. During his return voyage to the US, however, Congress amended the Chinese Exclusion Act so as to discontinue this policy of return vouchers. Subsequently, when Ping arrived at the port of San Francisco, he was refused reentry into the US. Ping sued to be readmitted on grounds that the amendment barring his reentry was *ex post facto* and therefore a violation of his rights. Ping's case eventually went to the Supreme Court, which ruled against him. According to Justice Field, who delivered the majority opinion, the reason Ping had no case against the US federal government was because:

the United States, through the action of the legislative department, can exclude [noncitizens] from its territory is a proposition which we do not think open to controversy. Jurisdiction over its own territory to that extent is an incident of every independent nation. It is a part of its independence. If it could not exclude [noncitizens] it would be to that extent subject to the control of another power.[4]

In other words, because the US is an independent nation (i.e., a sovereign regime), the federal government not only had the discretionary power to admit, but reciprocally also had the discretionary power to exclude nonciti- zens without judicial review. The matter of Ping's exclusion being *ex post facto* was therefore irrelevant to this case. Ping's presence in the US was always merely a privilege, not a right, which he enjoyed at the pleasure of the US federal government.

Four years after the *Chae Chan Ping* case, the *Fong Yue Ting v. United States* case (also known as the Geary Act case) went before the Supreme Court. At stake in this case was the constitutionality of the Geary Act, which had extended the Chinese Exclusion Act for an additional ten years and required persons of Chinese descent to acquire and carry iden- tification papers. Failure to acquire and carry such papers was punishable by deportation or one-year hard labor. Fong Yue Ting, an LPR since 1879, had never acquired identification papers and was subsequently arrested for violation of the Geary Act. Ting argued that because he was an LPR he was entitled to due process and therefore a hearing on the facts of the case before he could be deported.

The Court ruled against Ting because, besides having the discretionary power to admit and to exclude, the US federal government was also found to have the discretionary power to remove noncitizens. Justice Horace Gray, who delivered the majority opinion in the case, stated that: "The power of Congress . . . to expel, like the power to exclude [noncitizens], or any specified class of aliens, from the country, may be exercised entirely through executive officers. . . ."[5] Furthermore, the court ruled that deportation was not a punishment, so the due process protections of the Constitution did not apply to cases of deportation. As Gray reasoned:

> The order of deportation is not a punishment for crime. It is not a banishment, in the sense in which that word is often applied to the expulsion of a citizen from his country by way of punishment. It is but a method of enforcing the return to his own country of [a noncitizen] who has not complied with the conditions upon the performance of which the government of the nation, acting within its constitutional authority and through the proper departments, has determined that his continuing to reside here shall depend. He has not, therefore, been deprived of life, liberty or property, without due process of law; and the provisions of the Constitution, securing the right of trial by jury, and prohibiting unreasonable searches and seizures, and cruel and unusual punishments, have no application.[6]

This reasoning remained consistent three years later in another Chinese Exclusion Case, *Wong Wing v. United States.* In that case, Wong Wing was found to be in violation of the Chinese Exclusion Act and was sentenced to hard labor which would then be followed by his deportation to China.

Wong Wing objected that this was unconstitutional because his guilt was assessed without a trial-by-jury. The Supreme Court heard the case and ruled that the forced labor provision in Chinese Exclusion Act was indeed unconstitutional because it constituted a form of punishment, but the deportation aspect was not because it was not a punishment. In short, this case found that while most convictions obtained without a trial-by-jury were unconstitutional, it was not unconstitutional to deport noncitizens, including LPRs, without a trial-by-jury.[7]

While there are other Supreme Court cases that serve supplementary roles, these sets of cases—the *Passenger Cases* and the *Chinese Exclusion Cases*—together form the legal backbone of the US Plenary Power Doctrine. The US federal government, as a sovereign regime, is understood to have complete discretion in regulating immigration (i.e., admission, exclusion, and removal of noncitizens) and its exercise of power in this area is not subject to judicial review. The lack of judicial review means that, with regard to the admission, exclusion, and removal, noncitizens are without many essential constitutional protections (e.g., right to a trial-by-jury, right to court appointed legal representation, and freedom from unreasonable searches and seizures). In the following sections, I will make the case that this is a problematic conception of sovereignty and that we ought to reject this concept in favor of one that checks a political regime's ability to exercise this kind of discretionary power in any one area of government.

SOVEREIGNTY AS A RESPONSE TO THE STATE OF NATURE

In *Leviathan*, Thomas Hobbes famously made the case that security required the establishment of a unitary and absolute sovereign. In laying out his argument, Hobbes addressed three aspects of sovereignty: how political power is made legitimate, where it should be located, and to what degree it can be wielded.[8] With regard to the first, Hobbes argued that political power is legitimate only if those who will be subject to it would ideally consent to the arrangement, and at the same time, would not be put in a position that is worse than that characterized by the *state of nature*. As for the other two aspects of sovereignty, Hobbes believed that political power should be absolute, undivided and concentrated in the hands of one body.

Hobbes favored such a view of sovereignty because he felt that anything less would leave society in a *state of nature*, which he memorably described as a state where ". . . every man is enemy to every man . . . men live without other security than what their own strength and their own invention shall furnish them withal . . . and the life of man, solitary, poor, nasty, brutish, and short."[9] This, according to Hobbes, is because the *state of nature* is a state where everyone has a right to everything and everyone is equal in that anyone can potentially kill anyone else. In the *state of nature*, even the weakest, either by craft or by joining up with others, has the ability to kill the strongest.[10] For Hobbes this is the prototypical example of insecurity: a volatile situation where personal safety has no assurance.

To get out of this condition and prevent its reemergence, Hobbes argued that it would be necessary to enter into a state of peace. In fact Hobbes called this impulse the first and most fundamental law of nature: "Seek peace and follow it."[11] Yet, because of human nature, Hobbes believed people could only be compelled to do anything, including maintaining peace, if there was a power strong enough to coerce them or insure that others would follow through. As he writes: "before the names of just and unjust can have place, there must be some coercive power of some punishment greater than the benefit they expect by breach of their covenant."[12] In other words, a society that provides safety for individuals and is governed by the rule of law will only come into existence when there is a strong enough sovereign that can insure peace. Without such a powerful sovereign there is no guarantee that people can live peacefully, engage freely in trade, or enjoy any sense of personal safety.

For Hobbes, a regime with absolute authority and undivided power can only be legitimately established, however, through a social contract (i.e., the consensual agreement among potential subjects). As he writes:

> The only way to erect such a common power as may be able to [provide security] is [for the subjects] to confer all their power and strength upon one man, or upon one assembly of men . . . every man should say to every man *I authorize and give up my right of governing myself to this man, or to this assembly of men, on this condition, that thou give up thy right to him, and authorize all his actions in like manner.* . . . And he that carrieth this person is called Sovereign, and said to have *Sovereign Power.*[13]

This form of sovereignty was necessary, Hobbes believed, because the threat of the *state of nature* is ever-present and so must constantly be guarded against, even if such a state has never actually existed.[14] Such a sovereign therefore neutralizes the conditions that that threaten to destabilize society and/or the safety of individuals. As Hobbes notes:

> The Office of the sovereign, be it a monarch or an assembly, consisteth in the end, for which he was trusted with the sovereign power, namely the procuration of the safety of the people. . . . But by safety here, is not meant a bare preservation, but also all other contentments of life, which every man by lawful industry, without danger, or hurt to the commonwealth, shall acquire to himself.[15]

In considering how the Hobbesian framework would apply to the question of immigration, Phillip Cole has argued that there are two viable versions. The first is the external version, which holds that: "the international 'order' is a Hobbesian state of nature, in which liberal states are rare and vulnerable and are under constant danger from external and illiberal threats."[16] Because of these and/or other external threats, states are justified, independent of other considerations, in performing whatever actions promote their security. This includes having the discretionary right to control immigration.

The second is the internal account. According to this account "a policy of open borders would create such a level of instability that liberal institutions would be overwhelmed, and so on this particular question liberal states must have Hobbesian powers."[17] In other words, denying states the discretionary right to control immigration would have catastrophic internal consequences. For example, unrestrained immigration could threaten the current form of government (e.g., too many immigrants could lead to anarchy or regime change), social welfare (e.g., too many immigrants could undermine social trust and social safety nets), or threaten the safety of individuals (e.g., immigrants bring with them infectious diseases and proliferate crime).[18] Any of these possibilities could in turn produce an internal *state of nature*. According to Cole, both the external and internal concern with a *state of nature* share one common conclusion: ". . . individual states have the complete right to determine internal matters, such as immigration regulations, without external interference or constraint."[19]

Before simply conceding such powers to a political regime, however, there are at least three different objections that can be raised against the Hobbesian framework. The first is the liberal objection, which holds that a concern for liberty should take precedence over a concern for security. The philosopher John Locke is usually credited with articulating this response to Hobbes. On Locke's account the *state of nature* is not necessarily a "state of war," but a place where, at best, liberty reigns supreme and, at worst, is an inconvenient place to live.[20] Working with this conception of the *state of nature*, Locke did not believe that there could ever be a reason or need to grant any person, or body, such absolute powers.[21]

The second is the conservative objection to Hobbes, which best exemplified by David Hume and Edmund Burke.[22] This response holds that tradition and habit, not consent, provides political regimes with their legitimacy and stability. Therefore, according to this objection, Hobbes is right that security is the primary political concern, but is wrong in grounding its solution in the rational consent of individuals. On this account, the preservation of tradition does the work of providing security, so that is where the focus should be instead of on hypothetical social contracts.

The third objection to Hobbes, and the one I will focus on in the remainder of this chapter, is the *state of exception*. In the section that follows I will provide a much more developed account of this objection, but here I want to stress what it is that makes it different from the other two. First, as opposed to the liberal objection, the *state of exception* objection continues to make security, rather than liberty, its primary concern. This is important because if forced to choose between liberty and security, some are okay with trading their liberty for security. In those cases, the force of the Hobbesian framework, as either an external and internal justification for a political regime's discretionary right to control immigration, would continue to hold sway. I will return to the liberal objection in Chapter 2, but for the moment I will put the liberal objection to the side.

Unlike the conservative objection, and its commitment to maintaining stability through tradition, the *state of exception* objection is principally concerned with the lack of personal safety. In fact, this objection worries to that focusing too much on maintaining stability (e.g., law and order) can actually make individuals more vulnerable. According to the *state of exception* objection, Hobbes's notion of sovereignty does not so much ameliorate the threat to personal safety as much as it exacerbates it. In such cases, neither the external nor internal version of the *state of nature* would justify giving a political regime complete discretionary power over immigration because neither would provide the individual with more safety than he or she would find in a *state of nature*.

SOVEREIGNTY AS A STATE OF EXCEPTION

The contemporary Italian philosopher Giorgio Agamben best articulates this third objection to the Hobbesian framework by describing the situation as the "abandonment" of the subject. By *abandonment*, Agamben means a life that is no longer protected, but is exposed to the violence of the sovereign.[23] The classic example that Agamben provides in his book *Remnants of Auschwitz* is the fate of the "Muselman." The Muselman is the name given to persons in concentration camps, in particular Auschwitz, who live out an existence that ". . . one hesitates to call them living: one hesitates to call their death death."[24] Agamben's aim is to make the inverse case of Hobbes. Where Hobbes was preoccupied with the kind of insecurity a weak political regime invited, Agamben worries about the insecurity engendered by an overly legalistic and all-powerful political regime. In short, Agamben is pointing out that Hobbes's solution for getting out of the *state of nature* only modifies, but never resolves, the threat to security. Another way to put it is that the threat of a state of war, which is what originally motivated Hobbes's thinking, is only replaced on his account with the threat of abandonment.

In making his case, Agamben relies heavily on the work of Walter Benjamin. Agamben argues that Benjamin is prophetic in showing the link ". . . between the violence that posits law and the violence that preserves it."[25] Agamben is here articulating what he goes on to call the paradox of sovereignty: ". . . that the sovereign is, at the same time, outside and inside, the juridical order."[26] In other words, while the sovereign is the creator and enforcer of laws, it is not at the same time subject to those laws. This conception of sovereignty even predates Hobbes and might best be articulated in the work of sixteenth-century political theorist Jean Bodin, who writes that:

> the distinguishing mark of the sovereign [is] that he cannot in any way be subject to the commands of another, for it is he who makes law for the subject, abrogates law already made, and amends obsolete law. No one who is subject either to the law or to some other person can do this. That is why it is laid down in the civil law that the prince is above the law, for the word law in Latin implies the command of him who is invested with sovereign power.[27]

This ability to be both inside and outside the law is necessary for the sovereign to establish law and order, but that ability is also what makes a *state of exception* possible. As Carl Schmitt, whose conception of sovereignty Agamben is indebted to throughout *Homo Sacer* and *State of Exception*,[28] points out: "Sovereign is he who decides on the exception."[29] The exception provides the sovereign with a free hand to both identify a threat to the political regime and do what is necessary to address it as quickly as possible. This exception is supposed to be reserved for times of emergency, where the sovereign's ability to maintain law and order is in peril. Yet, what is supposed to be an exception has a tendency of becoming the norm, and thereby a security concern itself.

A specific example that Agamben gives is the use of Article 48 of the Weimar Constitution in 1933.[30] This article was originally aimed at dealing with an economic crisis, but instead it did far more. It led to a suspension of constitutional rights, gave Hitler and the fascists absolute power, and ultimately became part of the normal order of things instead of being merely an exception. According to Agamben, this is supposed to show how responding to the security concern by giving a regime absolute power can itself create the conditions that lead to as big, if not bigger, security concern than the one it is supposed to resolve.

Agamben is here raising a powerful, if not debilitating, challenge to the possibility of legitimate sovereignty. If we take Agamben's critique seriously, one conclusion that might be drawn is that we should dispense with notions of sovereignty altogether and instead resort to subverting, as much as possible, all forms of concentrated power and coercive authority. If we were to opt for this alternative, however, it seems that we would only be re-opening the problem we began with (i.e., *state of nature*). It seems that without a legitimate sovereign authority a political regime cannot maintain law and order, but with such power a political regime itself becomes a threat to individuals.

To summarize, it seems that Agamben brings us to a very unpleasant conclusion. Solutions to either part of the security concern—a stable and well-ordered society or personal safety—seem to be mutually exclusive. We might be able to get one, but not both. Therefore, we might never be able to fully address the security concern as a whole. This conclusion is what I refer to as the *security dilemma,* where we are left to choose between either the constant threat of a *state of nature* or a *state of exception*.

What does this mean for immigration policy? As already mentioned, the US federal government has enjoyed Plenary Power over immigration since at least the second half of the nineteenth century. Plenary Power allows the federal government to admit, exclude, and deport noncitizens as it sees fit. One way to understand this power is that, with regard to immigration, noncitizens have basically been *abandoned* by the US government and therefore live in a constant *state of exception*.[31] Most people should be aghast at this possibility and ought to think that justice demands that something be in place to protect *all* persons against such absolute and arbitrary exercises of power. As we saw in Section 1, however, the Courts have determined that limiting the discretion the US federal government has over matters of immigration could potentially undermine its legitimacy and leave the US in something akin to a *state of nature*.[32]

However, the unpleasant conclusion that this seems to leave us with—that the issue of immigration is forever stuck in a security dilemma—might not necessarily follow. In the remainder of this chapter, I argue that noncitizens, including undocumented immigrants, should be afforded more protections and that these protections would shield them from a *state of exception*. Furthermore, granting such protections also would not foreclose the possibility of a political regime having legitimate sovereignty. In fact, extending protections to noncitizens would be more consistent with the kind of sovereignty most political regimes now favor (eg., constitutional democracy). If this argument is successful, it would mean that avoiding the threat of the *state of exception* would not necessarily entail the possibility of falling into a *state of nature* or vice versa. In order to make this case, however, there are two horns that must be addressed. The next two sections will address each of these. First, Agamben's worry about the *state of exception* and then Hobbes's worry about the *state of nature*.

THE STATE OF EXCEPTION HORN OF
THE SECURITY DILEMMA

In this section, I defend the claim that an effective way to ameliorate many, if not all, the worries associated with a *state of exception* is through constitutional protections and judicial review. By constitutional protections I have in mind, at minimum, equal protection and due process under the law. By judicial review I have in mind that the coercive actions of a government should be, at minimum, subject to possible invalidation by an independent judiciary, especially when these actions go beyond the enumerated powers of the government or fail to protect the rights of individuals.

Since these two recourses are already available to US citizens, we might begin testing this claim by looking at how effective constitutional protections and judicial review have been to preclude a *state of exception* among citizens (e.g., reducing the lives of citizens to a condition reminiscent of Agamben's notion of *bare life*). If they fail to be effective in this case, which I consider to be the easiest test case, then my claim is wrong and there is no need to explore it any further. However, if they are effective in this case then my claim has at least a solid starting point. Ultimately, my claim will only be successful if and when it can show that constitutional protections and judicial review are enough to prevent a political regime from *abandoning* noncitizens, including those who have not been officially admitted by the regime (e.g., undocumented immigrants).

Support for the view that constitutional protections and judicial review can prevent a political regime from *abandoning* citizens can be found in the 1898 *United States v. Wong Kim Ark* case. In this case, Wong Kim Ark, who was born in San Francisco to Chinese parents, was returning to the US from a trip to China. In attempting to reenter the US, Ark was denied reentry on grounds that his citizenship had been revoked. As mentioned before, the *Chinese Exclusion Acts* had denied Chinese subjects the possibility of becoming US citizens, but there was no mention in the Act that this denial of citizenship extended to the children of Chinese subjects born in the US.

The reason is that all persons born in the US are automatically granted US citizenship at birth. This is clearly written in the first section of the Fourteenth Amendment and is known as the *Jus Soli* clause.

All persons born or naturalized in the United States, and subject to the jurisdiction thereof, are citizens of the United States and of the State wherein they reside. No State shall make or enforce any law which shall abridge the privileges or immunities of citizens of the United States; nor shall any State deprive any person of life, liberty, or property, without due process of law; nor deny to any person within its jurisdiction the equal protection of the laws.[33]

Therefore, at the heart of the *Wong Kim Ark* case was the question of whether the Fourteenth Amendment's *Jus Soli* clause extended to the children of noncitizens born in the US and whether citizenship obtained in this manner could be revoked by an act of congress.

By this point in US history, the Plenary Power Doctrine had already been established. If we recall, this meant that US courts could not hear cases involving matters of immigration policy. So before determining whether or not the *Jus Soli* clause would apply in this case, the Supreme Court first had to determine whether or not it could hear the case. The Court's conclusion was that the main issue of contention was not immigration, but citizenship and that these two issues were separate. This meant that the federal government's Plenary Power did not apply to this case.

The next question before the court was whether the federal government, beyond having a free hand in determining immigration policy, also had the discretionary right to grant, revoke, or suspend birthright citizenship. If it did, then in the federal government would indeed have a Schmitt-like power to decide on the exception (at least in cases involving citizenship). The Supreme Court, however, found that it did not. Wong Kim Ark had acquired US citizenship at birth, regardless of his parents' nationality or ineligibility for US citizenship, and it was not within the power of the federal government to deny, revoke, or suspend birthright citizenship. The Fourteenth Amendment's *Jus Soli* clause was, and continues to be, interpreted in this very strong manner—with no exceptions.

But while the federal government cannot revoke or suspend birthright citizenship, another question to consider is whether it is possible for the federal government to suspend or revoke naturalized citizenship. This was the question before the Supreme Court in the 1967 *Afroyim v. Rusk* case. In this case Beys Afroyim, a naturalized citizen from Poland, went to Israel and voted in an Israeli election. Later, when he reapplied for a US passport, the state department denied his request on grounds that he had lost his citizenship when he voted in the Israeli election. This rejection of citizenship was part of a stipulation in the *Nationality Act of 1940*, which stated that voting in an election outside of the US was sufficient to renounce one's US citizenship. Afroyim argued that this stipulation in the *Nationality Act of 1940* violated his right to due process and furthermore that while the US Constitution grants Congress exclusive power over the naturalization process, it does not give it the power to revoke citizenship once it has been acquired. The Supreme Court agreed with Afroyim stating that:

> we reject the idea . . . that . . . Congress has any general power, express or implied, to take away an American citizen's citizenship without his assent. This power cannot . . . be sustained as an implied attribute of sovereignty possessed by all nations.[34]

This ruling, therefore, further circumvented the US federal government's Plenary Power by emphatically stating that its discretion does not extend to any cases involving citizenship.

But while the Plenary Power Doctrine does not give the federal government the discretion to revoke or suspend citizenship, one might still ask if it is possible for the federal government to revoke or suspend citizenship through other means. For example, could the federal government revoke the citizenship of those who commit serious enough offenses? In this regard, the 1958 *Trop v. Dulles* case serves as an excellent example.

In *Trop v. Dulles* the US government attempted to strip Albert Trop of his US citizenship as part of his punishment for deserting the US Army. The Supreme Court ruled, however, that stripping individuals of their citizenship was a violation of their 8th Amendment right against cruel and unusual punishment. Chief Justice Warren, delivering the majority opinion, reasoned, in this long but important passage, that as a form of punishment taking away one's citizenship would constitute:

> the total destruction of the individual's status in organized society [and] is a form of punishment more primitive than torture. . . . The punishment strips the citizen of his status in the national and international political community. . . . In short, the expatriate has lost the right to have rights. . . . This punishment is offensive to cardinal principles for which the Constitution stands. It subjects the individual to a fate of ever-increasing fear and distress. He knows not what discriminations may be established against him, what proscriptions may be directed against him, and when and for what cause his existence in his native land may be terminated. He may be subject to banishment, a fate universally decried by civilized people. He is stateless, a condition deplored in the international community of democracies. It is no answer to suggest that all the disastrous consequences of this fate may not be brought to bear on a stateless person. The threat makes the punishment obnoxious.[35]

In this case we see that not only was the law was on the side of the potential *Muselmann* (Agamben's exemplar of *bare life*), but also worked against the sovereign, limiting and denying it the possibility of stripping a convicted army deserter of his political status.

These cases seem sufficient to show that constitutional protections and judicial review can be enough to prevent a political regime from reducing its citizens to a position paralleling Agamben's notion of *bare life*. These cases, however, have not yet shown that constitutional protections and judicial review can do the same with respect to noncitizens.[36] So the next question to address is whether constitutional protections and judicial review, if extended to noncitizens, would be enough to protect them from a political regime *abandoning* them? I think they can be and as evidence I cite four specific cases where the rights of noncitizens, including in some cases undocumented immigrants, took precedence over the explicit wishes of the sovereign.

The first of these cases is the 2010 *Padilla v. Commonwealth of Kentucky* case. In this case, Jose Padilla, an LPR from Honduras who had lived in the US for over forty years and had served in the US military during the Vietnam War, was charged with transporting marijuana. On the advice of his attorney, Padilla took a plea bargain and pleaded guilty to the charge. By pleading guilty, however, Padilla made himself subject to immediate removal under US federal immigration law. Padilla's lawyer, who did not have a strong grasp of US immigration law and the consequences a criminal conviction would entail, had erroneously believed that Padilla's military service and forty-plus years living in the US would shield him from deportation. This was not the case.

In a last-ditch effort to avoid being deported, Padilla filled a pro se motion alleging that his attorney's bad advice constituted a violation of his Sixth Amendment right to effective counsel. The Kentucky Supreme Court initially ruled against Padilla, arguing that his attorney was only required to inform him of direct consequences of a guilty plea (e.g., how much time he would serve in jail) and deportation was only a collateral effect. The view that immigration consequences are merely collateral effects can be traced back to the decisions we saw earlier in *Fong Yue Ting* and *Wong Wing*, where noncitizens were given protections from punishment, but not from deportation because deportation was not considered punishment.

The Supreme Court eventually took up Padilla's case and ruled in his favor. The Court concluded that, because of the seriousness of deportation, attorneys had a duty to effectively advise their clients on the immigration consequences of a guilty plea.[37] In short, *Padilla v. Commonwealth of Kentucky* showed (pace the rulings in *Fong Yue Ting* and *Wong Wing*) that Sixth Amendment protections could be invoked in immigration cases and that these protections could be effective in preventing the US federal government from deporting noncitizens.

But while this case tells us that deportation is a serious enough consequence such that noncitizens are owed some protections from it, it tells us very little about the rights that noncitizens have when they have been found removable in other cases. In this regard, the 2001 *Zadvydas v. INS* case is insightful. This case involves Kestutis Zadvydas, a noncitizen who in 1994 was given deportation orders because of various criminal convictions. Under normal circumstances, when a person is given final removal orders the US federal government has ninety days to deport them. In order to deport someone, however, there needs to be a country that is willing to take them and usually it's the country where they have citizenship. If the person is not deported in within those ninety days, the person is either entered into post-removal-proceedings (i.e., detention) or the person is set free.

The problem in Zadvydas's case was that there was no country that would take him. Zadvydas was born to Lithuanian parents in a displaced-persons camp in Germany. Because of Zadvydas unique situation, coupled with his criminal record, neither country would recognize him as one of their citizens or grant him admission. This essentially made the deportation of Zadvydas almost impossible. While there were no set limits on post-removal-proceedings, it was understood that detention could not go on indefinitely. Zadvydas therefore filed a writ of habeas corpus and demanded to be set free instead of indefinitely detained.

Zadvydas's case went before the Supreme Court where the question was whether the federal government has the power to indefinitely detain noncitizens in post-removal-proceedings. The Court's answer was no. According to Justice Breyer, who delivered the majority opinion of the Court:

> the statute, read in light of the Constitution's demands, limits an alien's post-removal-period detention to a period reasonably necessary to bring about that alien's removal from the United States [and] does not permit indefinite detention . . . once removal is no longer reasonably foreseeable, continued detention is no longer authorized by statute.[38]

Zadvydas was subsequently set free and his case continues to serve as a precedent under which certain removable noncitizens can avoid being deported.[39]

Zadvydas v. INS provides yet another example of how the threat of sovereign *abandonment*, even for noncitizens, can be curtailed through constitutional protections and judicial review. With that said, we need to bear in mind that Zadvydas, like Padilla, was a lawfully admitted immigrant who was never unlawfully present. So while constitutional protections and judicial review might protect all citizens and even lawfully admitted immigrants, could they do the same for immigrants who have not been officially admitted? If not, then undocumented immigrants might be said to be the exemplars of Agamben's notion of *bare life*. The following two cases, however, offer some reasons to think this is not the case.

The quintessential case with regard to the rights of undocumented immigrants is the 1982 *Plyer v. Doe* case. This case centered on the constitutionality of a 1975 Texas provision that would have withheld state funds from schools that enrolled children lacking proper immigration status. In this case, the Supreme Court ruled that the Texas provision violated the Fourteenth Amendment's equal protection clause. The Court found that undocumented immigrants fell under the category of "persons" and in denying persons an education the state was placing them at a severe disadvantage and would make them part of an underclass (i.e., would put them in something like an Agambenian *state of exception*). In striking down the Texas

provision, the Supreme Court set a precedent that is still in effect to this
day: all persons, including undocumented immigrants, must be allowed to
have access to such things as emergency medical care and public education
through the twelfth grade.[40]

Similar to the *Wong Kim Ark* case mentioned earlier, the Supreme Court
decided to hear the *Plyer v. Doe* case because it did not consider it an immigration case in the proper sense. So, while *Plyer v. Doe* might have established
that undocumented immigrants are owed some set of minimal protections, it
is still unclear whether they have any protections that would prevent a political regime from deporting them. In this regard, the 2005 *Clark v. Martinez* is
insightful.

The *Clark v. Martinez* case involved two unauthorized Cuban immigrants,
Daniel Benitez and Sergio Martinez, who entered the US through the now
infamous Mariel Boatlift of 1980. They were both later convicted of various
crimes. After serving their time in jail, the US federal government detained
Benitez and Martinez until they could be deported back to Cuba. Benitez
and Martinez, however, found themselves in a similar situation to Zadvydas;
their deportation was unforeseeable and so they found themselves indefinitely
detained. They argued that, just as in the case of Zadvydas, they should be
released. The problem, however, was that unlike Zadvydas they were never
officially admitted into the US. This might seem like minor difference, but
it had important repercussions. In the case of Zadvydas, the US federal government was prevented from deporting someone whom it had already let in.
The case of Benitez and Martinez was different because if they were released
the US federal government would have to take in immigrants whom it had
previously not admitted or wanted to admit. The Court ultimately sided with
Benitez and Martinez largely because they found that if it made no sense to
indefinitely detain removable aliens, it also made no sense to indefinitely
detain inadmissible aliens.[41] Because of the verdict in this case many "Mariel
Cubans" who had been in long-term detention were released.[42]

The arguments provided so far have not been meant to suggest that the
US Supreme Court is perfect, beyond reproach, and always on the side of
justice. Also, while these cases have made an impact on US immigration
detention and deportation practices, the truth is that the US continues to hold
thousands of migrants in detention centers under conditions very reminiscent
to the one's outlined by Agamben in *Homo Sacer*.[43] Still, I believe the larger
point of my claim holds true. *Pace* Agamben, constitutional protections and
judicial review are, at times, sufficient to protect the most vulnerable from the
coercive powers of a political regime. In fact, sometimes it's the *only thing*
that is protecting them.

Even if for the moment we grant that constitutional protections and judicial
review might be a way of ameliorating the concern with the *state of exception*,

we still have the second horn of the dilemma to deal with. Does extending constitutional protections and judicial review to all persons (including undocumented immigrants) in immigration cases not in turn undermine the sovereignty of a political regime? Well, it most certainly undermines things like the Plenary Power Doctrine, but as I will argue in the next section it does not necessarily undermine all forms of legitimate sovereignty.

THE STATE OF NATURE HORN OF THE SECURITY DILEMMA

In this section, I argue that extending constitutional protections and judicial review to noncitizens in immigration cases does not necessarily undermine, but in fact can be more consistent with certain understandings of sovereignty. In order to make this case, it is important to look more closely at the concept of sovereignty and see if in fact Hobbes's version is the only or best possible conception. My claim is that it's not and that constitutional democracy provides a better and more attractive alternative.

This exploration into the concept of sovereignty begins however not with Hobbes, but with his predecessor Jean Bodin. Bodin is usually credited with developing the modern notion sovereignty and the following passage from his 1576 *Six Books of the Commonwealth* provides us with both his definition and explanation of sovereignty:

> Sovereignty is that absolute and perpetual power vested in a commonwealth ... I have described it as perpetual because one can give absolute power to a person or group of persons for a period of time, but that time expired they become subjects once more. Therefore even while they enjoy power, they cannot properly be regarded as sovereign rulers, but only as the lieutenants and agents of the sovereign ruler, till the moment comes when it pleases the prince or the people to revoke the gift. The true sovereign remains always seized of his power. ... If it were otherwise, and the absolute authority delegated by the prince to a lieutenant was regarded as itself sovereign power, the latter could use it against his prince who would thereby forfeit his eminence, and the subject could command his lord, the servant his master. This is a manifest absurdity, considering that the sovereign is always excepted personally, as a matter of right, in all delegations of authority, however extensive. ... A perpetual authority therefore must be understood to mean one that lasts for the lifetime of him who exercises it.[44]

The key insight of this long passage is the distinction Bodin draws between a sovereign in the true sense and those who might, from time to time, enjoy political power. In his chapter "Binding Sovereigns," Daniel Deudney expands on this distinction by arguing that sovereignty, in the true sense of the term, has at least three parts: (1) How is political power legitimated as opposed to merely maintained? (2) Where is or should political power be located? (3) How should political power be wielded?[45]

As we saw in Section 2 of this chapter, Hobbes's answer to the first of these questions was that political power is legitimate only when everyone would ideally consent to it and would not be put in a more disadvantaged position then they would find in the *state of nature*. With regard to the second and third question, Hobbes's answer was that political power should be absolute, undivided, and concentrated in the hands of one person or body.[46] Deudney's point here is that, while Hobbes's conception of sovereignty has received most of the attention, it does not exhaust the possible range of conceptions of sovereignty.

Deudney does not take any issue with Hobbes's answer to the legitimacy question (i.e., question 1), which is that some form of consent is ultimately necessary in order for political power to be legitimate. Some would disagree with this view, as we saw in the conservative objection of Hume and Burke above, but we will table that discussion for Chapter 2 when we take up the conservative objection in full. Deudney's focus here is on the other two parts of sovereignty. With respect to the second question—where political power should be located—Deudney suggests there are two places where it could be located: with the state or with the people.[47] With regard to the third question—of how political power should be wielded—Deudney suggests another set of possibilities: political power can be engaged or recessed. With respect to engagement, Deudney states that: "The sovereign is engaged when it actually wields governmental authority" (e.g., a centralized form of government).[48] With respect to recessed: "The sovereign of a polity is recessed when the exercise of authority has been delegated to some other body or bodies" (e.g., a federalist form of government).[49]

While Deudney's account of sovereignty might not be exhaustive either, it at least shows how diverse and complicated the concept of sovereignty can be. If we stay just with Deudney's account, it would be possible to have up to four different types of legitimate sovereignty: an engaged state, a recessed state, an engaged public, and a recessed public.[50] Of the following, only the engaged state matches the Hobbes's conception, which Agamben rightfully criticizes on its own terms. Yet, there remain at least three different possible forms of legitimate sovereignty.

Deudney goes on to point out that an engaged state is usually exemplified by the kinds of regimes (i.e., nation-states) that arose after the 1648 Peace of Westphalia. Generally speaking, the Westphalia peace agreement is important in world history because it brought an end to the religious wars in Europe that ensued after the disintegration of the Holy Roman Empire and the social and political upheavals initiated by the Protestant Reformation (e.g., the questioning of the belief that the Pope is the highest authority in all of Christendom).

Without getting too much into the details of the Thirty Years War or its resolution, it is sufficient for our purposes to note two things. First, the Peace of Westphalia resolved, to some degree, the religious question that prompted the wars in Europe at this time. The question of what religion dominated in any given territory of Europe was answered by having all the parties involved agree to respect the doctrine of *cuius regio, eius religio.* This doctrine states that the ruler of the territory determines the religion. Secondly, this treaty gave rise to a system of nation-states that we now have taken for granted. After the Peace of Westphalia, nation-states—as opposed to religious leaders, nobles, or even kings—became recognized as the principle political actors on the world stage.

In contrast to this Westphalian model, there is what Deudney calls the Philadelphia model and it is supposed to exemplify a recessed public (e.g., a constitutional democracy). This alternative model is guided by the spirit of the 1776 US Declaration of Independence and is exemplified by the US Constitutional Convention of 1787. On this model, thirteen original colonies became one federalized state, which is considerably different from what would have happened if the US colonists had chosen to adopt a Westphalian model. Under a Westphalian model, the thirteen original colonies would have either become thirteen distinct states operating within a new state-system, as happened in Europe, or they would have conglomerated into one homogenous nation-state.

One reason why the US Constitutional Convention might have adopted a different model of sovereignty is that it arose under very different circumstances than those of seventeenth-century Europe. The New England colonists who rebelled in 1776 did so not because their sovereign had failed to provide them with security, but because their sovereign had unjustly infringed on their liberty. The concern for liberty, at least according to most accounts, was the driving force behind the US War for independence and the establishment of the US Constitution a decade later. The Westphalia model, on the other hand, was primarily concerned with putting an end to a state of war and less worried about questions of liberty.

If both of these models, Westphalian and Philadelphian, represent a form of legitimate sovereignty, then it seems that the concept of sovereignty is not exclusively reserved for addressing the security concern, as Hobbes and Agamben might have us believe. Instead, the concept of sovereignty can also be used to resolve the liberty concern, as the liberal and republican traditions within political philosophy have long maintained. If this is the case, then limiting constitutional protections and judicial review might in fact undermine, rather than preserve sovereignty, especially in cases where something like the Philadelphia model is adopted. Finally, this suggests that we might have found a form of legitimate sovereignty (i.e., a Philadelphia model of sovereignty) that can avoid both horns of the *security dilemma*. The question this still leaves unanswered, and which will be taken up in the next chapter, is whether this form of sovereignty is really sufficient to resolve the liberty concern?

CONCLUSION

Appealing to a Philadelphia model of sovereignty seems to raise a puzzle for my account. If the supposed basis for current US political regime is this model and not the Hobbesian one, then how is it that something like the Plenary Power Doctrine was able to come to fruition? Here it might be fruitful to take a slight detour and compare the *Chinese Exclusion Cases* with the 1896 *Plessy v. Ferguson* case (i.e., the separate-but-equal case). In doing so we will be better able to understand not only how something like the Plenary Power Doctrine arose, but more importantly why it is inconsistent with constitutional democracy.

The *Chinese Exclusion Cases* and the *Plessy v. Ferguson* case are linked together in many ways. For starters, the decision was rendered by the same court. A more insidious parallel, however, is that all of these cases were both attempts to circumvent the equal protection clause of the Fourteenth Amendment. For example, in *Plessy v. Ferguson*, the question before the Court was whether racial segregation, at least within state law, constituted an infringement on the privileges and protections afforded by the Fourteenth Amendment. The Supreme Court ruled that it did not and that segregation was constitutional.

The case itself involved Homer Plessy who was arrested on June 7, 1892 as part of a planned challenge to the *1890 Louisiana Separate Car Act*. Plessy, who was of mixed-race ancestry, was arrested when he took a seat in a "whites only" train car and refused to move to a car reserved for Blacks. Plessy's case went before the Supreme Court, where the Court agreed that the Fourteenth Amendment was intended to establish racial equality before the law. The Court concluded, however, that: ". . . in the nature of things [the Fourteenth Amendment] could not have been intended to abolish distinctions based upon color, or to enforce social, as distinguished from political equality, or a commingling of the two races unsatisfactory to either."[51] In other words, The Court ruled that having separate facilities for Blacks was consistent with the Fourteenth Amendment, so long as the facilities were equal to those of whites. This ruling set the precedent for the infamous Separate-But-Equal Doctrine, which condoned racial segregation not only on railroad cars, but also in schools and access to voting.

The *Plessy v. Ferguson* decision was eventually recognized as a grave and embarrassing injustice that that went against the principles of the US Constitution. The Separate-But-Equal Doctrine was officially overturned in the landmark 1954 case *Brown v. Board of Education*. In that case the Court concluded the following: ". . . we hold that the plaintiffs and others similarly situated for whom the actions have been brought are, by reason of the segregation complained of, deprived of the equal protection of the laws guaranteed by the Fourteenth Amendment."[52] The Separate-But-Equal Doctrine was therefore overturned because it was inconsistent with constitutional democracy and undermined its ideals. The type of racial segregation that the Separate-But-Equal Doctrine produced jeopardized the political equality owed to all citizens. In a constitutional democracy (i.e., a recessed public), where political authority rests with the people and political power is not concentrated in the hands of one body, jeopardizing the political equality of citizens not only undermines basic liberties, but also the self-checking mechanism that allows this form of sovereignty to function properly. Without this self-checking mechanism, those subject to a political regime would constantly have to worry about the possibility of a *state of exception*.

Much like the Separate-But-Equal Doctrine, the Plenary Power Doctrine is also the product of racism. It was born out of cases defending the *Chinese Exclusion Acts*, which have now been repealed and recognized as a horribly racist mistake.[53] One explanation for why the Separate-But-Equal Doctrine has been repealed and the Plenary Power Doctrine remains in place is that the former primarily effected citizens, while the later primarily effects noncitizens. This reasoning has a certain intuitive appeal: citizens should always be treated as political equals, while noncitizens—because they are situated differently—can (or should) be treated differently. After all, if sovereignty means anything, it means being self-determined, and what else could self-determination entail then for a political regime to have the discretionary right to admit, exclude, and deport noncitizens? If this is the case, then there is no contradiction in maintaining that in violating the political equality of citizens, the Separate-But-Equal Doctrine was unconstitutional, but the Plenary Power Doctrine, which does not violate the political equality of citizens, is not.

This would be the case only if constitutional democracy needed only to be concerned with the political value of self-determination, as is the case under Westphalian models of sovereignty. However, as we saw in Section 5, a Philadelphia model of sovereignty also needs to show respect for individual freedom and universal equality. Individual freedom and universal equality are not exclusively reserved for citizens, but as was shown in cases such as *Plyer v. Doe*, *Zadvydas v. INS*, *Clark v. Martinez*, and *Padilla v. Commonwealth of Kentucky* these principles are thought to extend to all persons.

My contention is therefore that the Plenary Power Doctrine, just like the Separate-But-Equal Doctrine, goes against the better principles of constitutional democracy. If this is the case, then there seem to be two options. Either constitutional democracy should be rejected and replaced with a form of sovereignty whose principles are consistent with something like the Plenary Power Doctrine or the Plenary Power Doctrine should be rejected and the principles of constitutional democracy defended. If we choose the former we will find ourselves back in a *security dilemma*. However, if we opt for the later—as I advocate we do—we will free ourselves from the *security dilemma*, but only to be trapped in a new difficulty. This new difficulty I term the "liberty dilemma." This dilemma centers on the tension between democratic self-determination, individual freedom, and universal equality. These commitments are all essential to a Philadelphia model of sovereignty and yet they do not always cohere well together.

In bringing this chapter to a close, I would like to stress that supporting constitutional democracy is not to deny that are problems in actual existing constitutional democracies. The aim of this chapter simply has been to highlight the *security dilemma*—the theoretical difficulties that arise when the security concern is given priority over the liberty concern—and propose that the way to resolve this dilemma is to prioritize the liberty concern over the security concern (i.e., to opt for a Philadelphia model of sovereignty as opposed to a Westphalian model). Unfortunately, as we will see in the next couple of chapters, giving priority to the liberty concern raises its own set of theoretical difficulties, which are exacerbated when philosophers try to deal with issues like immigration.

NOTES

1. The Constitution only, and very indirectly, mentions the issue of immigration twice. See "The Constitution of the United States," Article 1, Section 8, Clause 4, and Article 1, Section 9, Clause 1.

2. *Smith v. Turner; Norris v. Boston*, 48 U.S. 283 (1849).

3. "Chinese Exclusion Act of 1882," ch.126, 47th cong., 1st Sess. (1882).

4. *Chae Chan Ping v. United States*, 130 U.S. 581 (1889).

5. *Fong Yue Ting v. United States*, 149 U.S. 698 (1893).

6. Ibid.

7. *Wong Wing v. United States*, 163 U.S. 228 (1896).

8. I borrow this reading of Hobbes from Daniel Deudney, "Binding Sovereigns: Authorities, Structures, and Geopolitics in Philadelphian Systems," *State Sovereignty as Social Construct*, ed. Thomas Biersteker and Cynthia Weber (Melbourne, Australia: Cambridge University Press, 1996).

9. Thomas Hobbes, *Leviathan*, ed. Edwin Curley (Indianapolis: Hackett Publishing, 1994), 76.

10. Ibid., 74.

11. Ibid., 80.

12. Ibid., 89.

13. Ibid., 89.

14. Ibid., 117–119.

15. Ibid., 219.

16. Phillip Cole, *Philosophies of Exclusion: Liberal Political Theory and Immigration*, (Edinburgh, Great Britain: Edinburgh University Press, 2000), 165.

17. Ibid.

18. Different versions of each of these concerns can be found in Peter Brimelow, *Alien Nation: Common Sense About America's Immigration Disaster* (New York: Harper Perennial, 1996); Samuel Huntington, *Who Are We? The Challenges to America's National Identity* (New York: Simon & Schuster Paperbacks, 2004); and Ann Coulter, *Adios, America: The Left's Plan to Turn Our Country into a Third World Hellhole* (Washington, DC: Regnery Publishing, 2015).

19. Cole, *Philosophies of Exclusion*, 18.

20. John Locke, *Second Treaties of Government*, ed. C.B. Macpherson (Indianapolis: Hackett Publishing, 1980).

21. Ibid., 72.

22. See David Hume, "Of the Original Contract," *Political Writings*, ed. Stuart D. Warner and Donald W. Livingston (Indianapolis: Hackett Publishing, 1994), 164–181; Edmond Burke, *Reflections on the Revolution in France* (London: Penguin Books, 2004).

23. Giorgio Agamben, *Homo Sacer: Sovereign Power and Bare Life*, trans. Daniel Heller-Roazen (Stanford: Stanford University Press, 1998), 159.

24. Giorgio Agamben, *Remnants of Auschwitz: The Witness and the Archive*, trans. Daniel Heller-Roazen (New York: Zone Books, 1999), 44.

25. Ibid., 63.

26. Ibid., 15.

27. Jean Bodin, *Six Books of the Commonwealth*, trans. M.J. Tooley (Oxford: Blackwell, 1955), 29. It should be noted that this view of sovereignty is slightly different from Hobbes in the following way. For Hobbes, obtaining consent is an important feature of sovereignty, but for Bodin it is not. For Bodin: "the principal mark of sovereign majesty and absolute power is the right to impose laws generally on all subjects regardless of their consent" (Bodin, *Six Books of the Commonwealth*, 33).

28. Giorgio Agamben, *State of Exception*, trans. Kevin Attell (Chicago: The University of Chicago Press, 2005), 1.

29. Carl Schmitt, *Political Theology* (Chicago: The University of Chicago Press, 1985), 5.

30. Agamben, *State of Exception*, 14–16.

31. For one of the clearest articulations of this view see Nicholas De Genova, "The Deportation Regime: Sovereignty, Space, and the Freedom of Movement," in *The Deportation Regime: Sovereignty, Space, and the Freedom of Movement*,

ed. Nicholas De Genova and Nathalie Peutz (Durham, NC: Duke University Press, 2010), 33–65.

32. Agamben would likely be a little unhappy with the framing of this paragraph as he would note that, while noncitizens are abandoned, they merely represent the potential that we all face of becoming abandoned. In other words, just because citizens technically have Constitutional rights at the moment, it does not mean that these rights cannot be thrown out in a state of exception. The argument I am putting forth here is therefore much more conservative than Agamben would like.

33. U.S. Const. am. 14., sec 1.

34. *Afroyim v. Rusk*, 387 U.S. 253 (1967).

35. *Trop v. Dulles*, 356 U.S. 86, 70 (1958).

36. For example, Nicholas De Genova has persuasively argued that Elvira Arellano—an undocumented immigrant who took sanctuary in a church for over a year in an effort to avoid final deportation orders—provides us with one of the clearest examples of *bare life*. See De Genova, "The Deportation Regime," 36–38.

37. *Padilla v. Commonwealth of Kentucky*, 559 U.S. 356 (2010).

38. *Zadvydas v. Davis*, 533 U.S. 678 (2001).

39. Jon Feere, "Reining in Zadvydas v. Davis: new bill aimed at stopping release of criminal aliens," *Center for Immigration Studies* May 2011, accessed August 15, 2014, http://www.cis.org/stopping-release-of-criminal-aliens

40. *Plyler v. Doe*, 457 U.S. 202 (1982).

41. *Clark v. Martinez*, 543 U.S. 371 (2005).

42. William R. Yates, "Memorandum For Regional Directors District Directors National Benefits Center Director Officers In Charge," March 7, 2005, accessed August 15, 2014, http://www.uscis.gov/sites/default/files/USCIS/Laws/Memoranda/Static_Files_Memoranda/Archives%201998–2008/2005/mariels030705.pdf

43. For an excellent account of the injustice and cost of US immigration detention practices see Todd Miller, *Border Patrol Nation: Dispatches from the Front Lines of Homeland Security*, (San Francisco: City Lights Books, 2014), 213–241.

44. Bodin, *Six Books of the Commonwealth*, 25–27.

45. See Daniel Deudney, "Binding Sovereigns: Authorities, Structures, and Geopolitics in Philadelphian Systems," *State Sovereignty as Social Construct*, ed. Thomas Biersteker and Cynthia Weber (Melbourne, Australia: Cambridge University Press, 1996).

46. Hobbes, *Leviathan*, 110–118.

47. Daniel Deudney, "Binding Sovereigns: Authorities, Structures, and Geopolitics in Philadelphian Systems," *State Sovereignty as Social Construct*, ed. Thomas Biersteker and Cynthia Weber (Melbourne, Australia: Cambridge University Press, 1996), 196.

48. Ibid.

49. Ibid.

50. Ibid., 197

51. *Plessy v. Ferguson*, 163 U.S. 537 (1896).

52. *Brown v. Board of Education of Topeka*, 347 U.S. 483 (1954).

53. The *Chinese Exclusion Act* was officially repealed by the *1943 Magnuson Act*, but it was not until the passage of the *Immigration and Nationality Act of 1965* that its last vestiges were removed.

Chapter 2

The Liberty Concern and
the Liberty Dilemma

In the previous chapter, I provided a brief outline of what I call the security concern. This outline began by summarizing Thomas Hobbes's response to the theoretical threat posed by a *state of nature* and then turned to the work of Giorgio Agamben, who argued that Hobbes's solution to this threat only produced a far worse condition than could ever be found in a *state of nature* (i.e., the *state of exception*). This objection to Hobbes seemed to leave us in a *security dilemma*: a situation in which responding to the threat of a *state of nature* only produced conditions conducive to a *state of exception*. With regard to immigration, I claimed that this dilemma is currently exemplified in the US Plenary Power Doctrine. I suggested that the Plenary Power Doctrine should be rejected, similar to the way the Separate-But-Equal Doctrine was rejected, and that doing would not necessarily lead to a Hobbesian *state of nature*. My defense of this claim rested on the possibility of there being at least one other option for legitimate sovereignty that could address both horns of the *security dilemma*. I maintained that by prioritizing the liberty concern, a Philadelphia model of sovereignty could provide such an alternative.

At the end of the chapter, however, I hinted at a potential problem with this solution. This is a problem that moral and political philosophers have had to grapple with from Locke to Rawls. The problem is that, much like the security concern, the liberty concern has its own internal tension. This tension consists in trying to reconcile a commitment to democratic self-determination with individual freedom and universal equality. All three of these commitments are essential to a Philadelphia model of sovereignty, yet because each appeals to competing notions of liberty they do not always cohere well together. This tension both poses a problem for the conclusion put forth at the end of Chapter 1 and also describes the dilemma philosophers working on the issue of immigration find themselves in.

This chapter therefore aims to do two things. First, trace the origin of the *liberty dilemma* through the work of philosophers that have exemplified the different positions one can take in an effort to address the liberty concern: the classical liberalism of John Locke, the civic-republicanism of Jean-Jacques Rousseau, and the conservatism of David Hume. I will then suggest that Immanuel Kant's account of autonomy ultimately provides the correct blueprint for overcoming the *liberty dilemma*. Kant's own account, however, has certain shortcomings, which are exposed by his utilitarian and Marxist critics. I conclude this chapter by looking at the work of John Rawls and arguing that his two principles of justice help supplement Kant's account by addressing those worries while maintaining the core of Kant's resolution to the *liberty dilemma*. If this account proves successful, then it would show that it is possible to have a legitimate form of sovereignty that avoids both the *liberty* and *security dilemmas*.

LOCKE AND THE CLASSICAL LIBERAL OPTION

As briefly mentioned in Chapter 1, John Locke's *Second Treatise of Government* provides one of the most compelling arguments against Hobbes.[1] Part of the attraction of Locke's account is that its based on a different understanding of human nature or, to put it another way, on a different understanding of what human beings would be like in the absence of government (i.e., the state of nature). According to Locke, there is no reason to believe that in the absence of government human beings would automatically find themselves is a state of war, which is a central assertion in Hobbes's account. Instead, Locke believed that the state of nature was a place where natural liberty (i.e., anarchy in the non-pejorative sense of the term) reigned supreme, but where it would quickly be an inconvenient place to live as institutions, such as private property, began to arise.[2]

Locke, therefore, has a more optimistic view of human nature, which is why it is so difficult for him to see what reason or need could arise that would warrant giving any person, or body, absolute political power. Despite Hobbes's depictions of doom and gloom, the actual insecurity presented by the state of nature was never for Locke severe enough to justify the kinds of restrictions on individual freedom that a Hobbesian sovereign would entail. For Locke, a life without liberty would be far worse than anything the state of nature had to offer. As Locke writes:

> It cannot be supposed that [those who enter into the social contract] should intend. . . to give to any one, or more, an absolute arbitrary power over their persons and estates, and put a force into the magistrate's hand to execute his unlimited will arbitrarily upon them. This were to put themselves into a worse condition than the state of nature.[3]

In summary, the Lockean objection to Hobbes is that it would be more rational to choose to stay in a state of nature, which on Locke's account is only an inconvenient place to live, than to subject oneself to the arbitrary and undivided power of an absolute sovereign.

Locke's objection might appear similar to Agamben's, but there is an important philosophical difference between the two. For Agamben, the complaint against Hobbes was that his notion of sovereignty did not resolve the issue of insecurity. Instead, the Hobbesian notion of sovereignty merely altered the security threat. On Agamben's account, the security threat morphs from a *state of nature* to a *state of exception*. Locke's account, on the other hand, is radically different in kind. Locke does not make security his primary concern. For Locke, liberty is the primary concern and it must be defended against the potential of arbitrary forms of coercion (e.g., the Hobbesian notion of sovereign).

Given their divergent starting points, it is not surprising that Locke's account of the social contract is much different than the one proposed by Hobbes. For Hobbes, the social contract aimed to establish peace and did so by creating a third party, the sovereign, who would be given political power as an irrevocable gift.[4] For Locke, the social contract gives rise to a regime where political power is held in trust and is subject to be revoked if the regime overreaches or misuses its power. As Locke states:

> there can be but *one supreme power* . . . [yet] there remains still *in the people a supreme power to remove or alter the* [sovereign], when they find the [sovereign's actions] contrary to the trust reposed in them: for all *power given with trust* for the attaining an *end* [and] whenever that *end* is manifestly neglected, or opposed, the *trust* must necessarily be *forfeited*, and the power devolve into the hands of those that gave it, who may place it anew where they shall think best for their safety and security.[5]

The important difference then is that Locke's account is not so much worried about peace and in fact suggests entering into a state of war if necessary to depose a tyrannical regime.[6] For Hobbes, on the other hand, revolts were only justified in very exceptional cases, such as when one's life had been put in immediate danger by the sovereign (e.g., when one has been sentenced to death by the state).

As already hinted at in Chapter 1, the reason legitimate revolts are largely absent from Hobbes's account is that he was primarily concerned with establishing peace (i.e., getting out of a state of war) and he was willing to sacrifice individual freedom in order to accomplish this task. Therefore, so long as the actions of a regime were aimed at establishing or maintaining peace, it is nearly impossible on Hobbes's account for it to overreach its sovereign powers. For Locke, the opposite was the case. "The great and *chief end* [of the sovereign] . . . is *the preservation of [an individual's] property*,"[7] which in Chapter 5 of the *Treatise* he already defined as an extension of individual freedom.[8] Therefore, on Locke's version of the social contract, individuals can never give up their freedom (i.e., rights given to them by God), but instead government is established in order to more efficiently and effectively protect it.

Locke's view exemplifies what most people call the classical liberal position. This position rests on the view that individuals are fundamentally free and that citizens should be provided with as many protections from government as possible. These protections include things such as basic liberties and respect for private property, but do not necessarily include what we might call entitlements (e.g., welfare benefits). The classical liberal notion of citizenship is therefore not very robust or demanding. So long as someone is subject to the coercive power of a regime, they are citizens who are entitled to basic rights and duties, which the regime is obligated to enforce and protect.

This notion of liberty, however, is not the only notion of liberty. There is another more robust notion of liberty that come from the civic-republican tradition. The difference between the two notions can be expressed as a difference between positive and negative liberty, a distinction usually credited to political theorist Isaiah Berlin. In his essay, "Two Concepts of Liberty," Berlin argued that negative liberty ". . . is the area within which the subject— a person or group of persons—is or should be left to do or be what he is able to do or be, without interference by other persons."[9] In other words, liberty in the negative sense is a lack of restrictions and nothing more.

In contrast, positive liberty requires the presence of something, as opposed to its mere absence. This latter type of liberty is championed by the civic-republican tradition. This view of liberty holds that an individual is self-determined or has self-mastery (i.e., autonomy) to the extent that they are active in civic life. Conversely, it also holds that there are certain forms of oppression and domination that can be addressed only through empowerment and not just the removal of restrictions. Liberty in this positive sense would therefore not be possible without some help or support from the community. This in turn leads to a much more robust notion of citizenship, one that goes beyond being left alone to one that aims to make citizens actively engaged in the process of self-government.

I will say more about the positive notion of liberty in the next section, but here it is important to note that we have found the kernel of the *liberty dilemma*: constitutional democracy (i.e., a Philadelphia model of sovereignty) requires liberty in both the positive (i.e., self-determination) and negative (i.e., individual freedom) sense, yet these two senses of liberty do not always cohere well together. While civic-republicans advocate for a positive notion of liberty as a means to promote engaged citizenship, classical liberals worry that such a notion will lead to an overly intrusive government that threatens the negative liberty of individuals. In the next section, I will explore this tension even more by outlining the civic-republicanism of Jean-Jacques Rousseau.

ROUSSEAU AND THE TWO HORNS
OF THE LIBERTY DILEMMA

Much like Hobbes and Locke, Jean-Jacques Rousseau's political philosophy begins with an assumption about human nature, that is expressed in a story about the original state of nature. Out of the three, Rousseau's account is by far the most optimistic. He posits that in the original state of nature humans are good and compassionate creatures who are only corrupted with the introduction of social and political institutions. According to Rousseau, these institutions corrupt humans by aggravating unnatural inequalities that in turn become fetters on natural liberty. This is succinctly expressed in Rousseau's often-quoted opening line to *The Social Contract*: "Man is born free, and everywhere he is in chains."[10]

Rousseau's critique of Hobbes is similar to Locke's in that he also rejects Hobbes's subordination of the liberty concern to the security concern. Rousseau's criticism, however, is based on a different set of worries. As mentioned above, Locke argued that those subject to a Hobbesian sovereign would not be made better off, but in fact would find themselves in a situation far worse than they would be in a state of nature. Rousseau's civic-republican critique of Hobbes's goes in a different direction, which also extends to Locke. Rousseau's complaint centers on the notion of consent and in particular why people consent to institutions that enslave rather than empower them.

Rousseau's answer to this apparent paradox is found in his *The Discourse on the Origin of Inequality*. In that work, Rousseau postulates that the reason people tacitly consent to relationships of domination is because they appear as extensions of natural inequalities. In other words, they appear as inequalities that cannot properly be consented to or rejected, sort of like an inequality in height. Rousseau argues that when the social contract gets forged, various unnatural inequalities get baked in as though they were natural givens. These inequalities turn out to greatly over-determine people's life chances and yet are not natural. As Rousseau writes: ". . . among the distinctive differences between men there are several that pass for natural but are solely the work of habit and the various ways of life that men adopt in society."[11] For Rousseau, most of the inequalities that undergird oppressive social and political institutions are of this unnatural type. In other words, the conditions of contemporary domination are not so much the byproduct of natural differences or explicit government coercion, but are the result of tacitly accepting unnatural inequalities as though they were fixed and unchanging.

If Rousseau is correct, then sovereign legitimacy requires more than mere tacit consent. It also requires that the unnatural inequalities, which were baked into the original social contract, get corrected.[12] On this point, Rousseau is not only critiquing Hobbes, but also Locke who famously argued that tacit consent was sufficient to legitimize political power.[13] In short, the primary concern of politics for Rousseau is neither insecurity nor restrictions on individual freedom, but the domination that results from unnatural inequalities. As Rousseau concludes in *The Discourse on the Origin of Inequality*:

> Such was [Hobbes and Locke's social contract], which gave new fetters to the weak and new forces to the rich, irretrievably destroyed natural liberty, established forever the law of property and of inequality, changed adroit usurpation into an irrevocable right, and for the profit of a few ambitious men henceforth subjected the entire human race to labor, servitude and misery.[14]

In other words, despite whatever differences there might be between the social contracts of Hobbes and Locke, they are both simply a validation of the old Thrasymachian thesis: justice is a sham designed by the powerful to convince the weak to obey laws that work against their own best interest and promote the advantages of the powerful.

Rousseau's attempt to provide a corrective account to the original social contract is found in a different text entitled *The Social Contract*. In that text, Rousseau begins, as all prior theories of social contracts do, by postulating an original state of nature that underwrites a particular theory of human nature. As already suggested, Rousseau's view of human nature is by far the most optimistic of the three. Rousseau writes glowingly that: "nothing is so gentle as man in his primitive state, when, placed by nature at an equal distance from the stupidity of brutes and the fatal enlightenment of civil man."[15]

For Rousseau, people in the state of nature are equally free and not under any threat from others. This natural liberty is jeopardized, however, with an increase in the human population. This increase eventually forces humans to both depend on and compete with each other. This dependence and competition brings into existence social and political institutions that put an end to the original state of nature. As Rousseau writes: "as soon as one man needed the help of another, as soon as one man realized that it was useful for a single individual to have provisions for two, [this state of nature] disappeared, property came into existence, labor became necessary."[16]

Once the original state of nature goes out of existence—and here Rousseau's view differs significantly from that of Hobbes and Locke—it can never return.

[T]he soul and human passions are imperceptibly altered and . . . change their nature . . . with original man gradually disappearing, society no longer offers to the eyes of the wise man anything but assemblage of artificial men and factitious passions which . . . have no true foundation in nature.[17]

With no way to get back to the original state, we have no recourse to natural freedom, meaning freedom as a lack of restrictions and therefore in the negative sense. The project of forging a social contract of nondomination becomes a task of ". . . taking men as they are [which is no longer in the original state of nature] and laws as they might be."[18]

Given the current state of humanity, Rousseau believes that the best that can be hoped for is a social contract that stresses liberty in the positive sense. As Rousseau explains:

What man loses through [a] social contract [of non-domination] is his natural liberty and an unlimited right to everything that tempts him and that he can acquire. What he gains is civil liberty and the propriety ownership of all he possesses. So as not to be in error in compensations, it is necessary to draw a careful distinction between natural liberty (which is limited solely by the force of the individual), and civil liberty (which is limited by the general will) . . . which alone makes him truly the master of himself. For to be driven by appetite alone is slavery, and obedience to the law one has prescribed for oneself is liberty.[19]

Rousseau's notion of the "general will" probably represents one of the most extreme examples of democratic self-determination found in all of Western philosophy. According to Rousseau, under the auspices of the *general will*, a people's right to self-determination will at times require that the desires of particular individuals conform to the interest of the whole such that, as Rousseau famously put it, individuals will sometimes ". . . be forced to be free."[20] The conditions necessary for this type of democratic self-determination might seem rather authoritarian, but for Rousseau this is how some semblance of liberty (i.e., prescribing the law to oneself) can be maintained in conditions where everyone is both dependent on others and have competing interests.

As can be gathered from his criticisms of Hobbes and Locke, the kind of positive liberty that Rousseau is advocating relies heavily on a notion of universal equality, which he explains in the following passage:

Regarding equality, we need not mean by this word that degrees of power and wealth are to be absolutely the same, but rather that, with regard to power, it should transcend all violence and never be exercised except by virtue of rank and laws; and with regard to wealth, no citizen should be so rich as to be capable of buying another citizen, and none so poor that he is forced to sell himself . . . Equality is said to be a speculative fiction that cannot exist in practice. But if abuse is inevitable, does it follow that it should not at least be regulated? It is precisely because the force of things tends always to destroy equality that the force of legislation should always tend to maintain it.[21]

So where Hobbes would design a political regime so as to address the problem of insecurity, and Locke would design it to maximize individual freedom, this last passage suggests that Rousseau would design a political regime so as to promote universal equality. For Rousseau, addressing inequality takes precedence because it is both a principle source of potential insecurity (e.g., class conflict) and creates the conditions that make a loss of liberty (e.g., de facto slavery) possible.

A common worry about Rousseau's view is that his solution to the liberty concern (i.e., the *general will*) might entail too strong a sense of collectivism. For example, Rousseau says that one is truly free even though they might be asked at any moment to sacrifice their own individual interests for the common good. Rousseau's social contract therefore represents the second horn of the *liberty dilemma*: civic-republicanism is able to recover a sense of democratic self-determination by promoting universal equality, but it does so at the expense of individual freedom.

We have now outlined both horns of the *liberty dilemma*: classical liberalism promotes individual freedom through its notion of negative liberty, but only at the expense of universal equality and democratic self-determination; civic-republicanism promotes democratic self-determination and universal equality through its notion of positive liberty, but only at the expense of individual freedom. The Philadelphia model of sovereignty, which offered a solution to the *security dilemma*, depends on both these notions of liberty, so requires a resolution to the *liberty dilemma*.

HUME AND THE CONSERVATIVE REPLY TO THE SOCIAL CONTRACT TRADITION

The *liberty dilemma* is also not the only problem that arises when the liberty concern is given priority over the security concern. Another issue to consider is whether and to what degree political legitimacy actually depends on the consent of those ruled. As we have seen above, all three social contract theorists, despite their differences, agreed that to some degree the consent of those ruled was necessary for a political regime to be legitimate. This is a basic assumption of social contract theory. However, this assumption is susceptible to a criticism leveled by David Hume. In a nutshell, Hume does not believe that the legitimacy of a political regime is derived from the consent of the people, but instead from the traditions, customs, and habits of that particular community.

Hume came to this conclusion in his attempt to resolve the political factionalism that plagued the politics of his day. For Hume, political factions had various sources, but the most pernicious were those that arose from what he called "abstract speculative principles."[22] For Hume, the two most insidious speculative political principles were (1) the belief in the divine right of kings and (2) the belief that government was founded upon the consent of the people.[23] I will mainly focus on the latter, because the first is now widely discredited, while the second presents an interesting challenge not only to social contract theory, but also to my claim that there can be a legitimate form of sovereignty that addresses both the security and liberty concern and at the same time does not fall into either a *liberty* or *security dilemma*.

As already mentioned, Hobbes, Locke, and Rousseau believed that in order for a political regime to be legitimate it must have the consent of those who will be subject to its authority. In his essay entitled "Of the Original Contract," Hume rejects this notion by making the following observation:

> Almost all the governments, which exist at present, or of which there remains any record in story, have been founded originally, either on usurpation or conquest, or both, without any pretence of a fair consent, or voluntary subjection of the people.[24]

Taking it one step further, Hume observes that not only are most regimes founded on usurpation or conquest, but also the idea that political legitimacy somehow depends on the consent of its subjects is relatively new. This is a problem for the social contract tradition because it strongly believes legitimacy is based on reason. If it is based on reason, then Hume is asking why has this idea not had much traction before the eighteenth century? As Hume writes: "It is strange, that an act of the mind, which every individual is supposed to have formed . . . should be so much unknown to all of them, that, over the face of the whole earth, there scarcely remain any traces or memory of it."[25] In short, Hume is raising two strong and interrelated objections to social contract theory. First, he denies that consent is necessary to make political power legitimate. Second, that establishing and maintaining law and order (i.e., address the security concern) is actually best achieved by appealing to tradition, custom, and habit.

Hume's objections to the social contract tradition depend on the view that justice is an artificial virtue as opposed to a natural one. This view of justice does not necessarily imply that justice is somehow unimportant or unreal. Rather, Hume is saying that justice, while consistent with and arising from, is not one of the original dispositions found in humans. For Hume, justice finds its origins in ". . . the selfishness and confined generosity of men, along with the scanty provision nature made for his wants . . ."[26] That is, humans have certain selfish interests (e.g., food, clothing, and shelter), but—and here we find some agreement with Rousseau—those interests are such that no one individual can adequately satisfy them alone. Furthermore, it turns out that the most effective way for individuals to meet these selfish interests is by forming and maintaining a society.[27]

A society cannot arise or be maintained, however, without some sense of justice, or more specifically, a respect for private property, as Hume notes: ". . . without justice, society must immediately dissolve, and every one must fall into that savage and solitary condition, which is infinitely worse than the worst situation that can possibly be supposed in society."[28] Here it appears as though Hume is coming fairly close to the Hobbesian view, but what differentiates him from Hobbes—and in fact from the whole of the social contract tradition—is his rejection of the idea that justice arises from or is based on some kind of promise or contract. According to Hume, the notion of a promise or contract cannot be the source of justice because they are already based on some prior conception of justice. For Hume, this reveals a vicious circularity at the heart of social contract tradition. In their accounts of justice, social contract theorists claimed to provide the moral underpinnings for notions such as promise and contract (i.e., a theory of justice), yet these same theorists appear to be relying on those same notions in accounting for the origin of justice.

As a way of avoiding this kind of vicious circular reasoning, Hume makes the case that our conception of justice actually arises from "the general sense of common interest"[29] or from the realization that it is in the best interest of all to do certain things, even when those things are not in our immediate self-interest. In those cases, our natural disposition to promote our immediate self-interest can be restrained by the understanding that in the long run we will benefit by acting against our own self-interest in these particular cases and this understanding begins to inculcate a habit in us of calling such actions "just." For Hume, this does not mean that justice is something we can simply ignore when it does not serve our immediate interest, but neither is it something that has meaning beyond a system of private property.

In opposition to social contract theorists, Hume argues that something like the following is probably a more likely account of how political regimes come to obtain legitimacy:

Time, by degrees, removes all these difficulties, and accustoms the nation to regard, as their lawful or native princes, that family, which, at first, they considered as usurpers or foreign conquerors. In order to found this opinion, they have no recourse to any notion of voluntary consent or promise, which, they know, never was, in this case, either expected or demanded. The original establishment was formed by violence, and submitted to from necessity. The subsequent administration is also supported by power, and acquiesced in by the people, not as a matter of choice, but of obligation. They imagine not, that their consent gives their prince a title: But they willingly consent, because they think, that, from long possession, he has acquired a title, independent of their choice or inclination.[30]

In other words, what binds subjects to their rulers and the reason they fulfill their obligations as citizens (i.e., obey the law and maintain public order) is that, at best, it is in their interest to do so and, at worst, it is done simply out of habit. Because of this, those who presently hold political power—regardless of how they originally came into it, which Hume openly admits was most likely through an act of usurpation or conquest—have a distinctive advantage in maintaining this power. The advantage stems from the likelihood that removing them from power would have worse consequences than simply leaving them in power.[31] This brings us back to Hume's original warning against political factions based on "abstract speculative principles." Such principles, for Hume, are myths that have no ground in reality and in being dogmatically committed to these mythological principles political factions form and disrupt social stability.

In summary, Hume's objection to social contract theory is that an original contract is impossible on both empirical and logical grounds. Empirically, there is no historical evidence to support the idea that political regimes have been or will be legitimated through something like a social contract. Logically, the type of legitimation required by something like a social contract is based on circular reasoning. The binding force of the social contract only makes sense within an already established civil society (i.e., a place where notions such as "mutual exchange" and "fair play" already have currency), yet this is exactly what the social contract is supposed to bring into existence. So instead of providing us with some moral and political insights into the nature of justice, social contract theory, at best, provides us with an unattainable fiction and, at worst, presents us with dangerous ideas that tend to lead to social disruption rather than stabilization. Instead, Hume urges his readers to strengthen the glue that really holds a society together: custom, habit, and tradition. *But where do those things come from?*

KANT'S ACCOUNT OF AUTONOMY

If no adequate philosophical response can be given to both the *liberty dilemma* and Hume's conservative objection, then the alternative proposed in Chapter 1 for dealing with the *security dilemma* (i.e., constitutional democracy) might not be able to get off the ground. In an effort to meet this challenge, this section turns to the work of Immanuel Kant and his notion of autonomy. This notion of autonomy is rooted in Kant's moral philosophy, but as we will see it also has important implications for his political theory as well.

According to Kant, the failing of most moral theories is that they are grounded on something external to what he calls the "will," for example they are grounded in either notions of happiness, divine perfection, or the threat of damnation. Over and against these heteronymous views, Kant argued that the autonomy of the will is the supreme principle of morality. By autonomy of the will Kant meant that, as free rational beings, we give (i.e., legislate) the moral law to ourselves, and this is what binds us to morality, not external effects or inclinations. Morality for Kant is therefore not conditional or grounded in sentiment, but is to be ". . . sought a priori solely in the concepts of pure reason."[32] Kant here is specifically rejecting Hume's claim that reason is the slave of the passions and that morality is derived from the sentiments alone, in particular the sentiments of self-interest and altruism.[33]

Kant's concept of morality has three essential parts that get articulated in his different formulations of the categorical imperative. The first formulation of the categorical imperative states that one should "Act only according to that maxim whereby you can at the same time will that it should become a universal law."[34] This is the universal part of Kant's moral theory. Morality demands a kind of law under which all cases may be subsumed, as opposed to a set of ad hoc rules or regulations that function only in particular cases. Kant objected to the idea that morality could be derived solely from experience, as Hume and other empiricists suggest, because experience only provides us with particular instances and never with general or universal laws.

This leads to the second part of his moral theory, which is that morality is derived from, and has as its final end, rationality itself (i.e., rationality is an "end-in-itself"). For Kant, humanity is rational nature and this is expressed in his second formulation of the categorical imperative: "Act in such a way that you treat humanity, whether in your own person or in the person of another, always at the same time as an end and never simply as a means."[35] In other words, we may never treat ourselves or any other person as a mere tool, object, or means toward some other end. Though we often treat others as a means—for example, when we someone performs a service for us—if we fail to recognize that person as also an end-in-themselves, we violate this moral law. We must therefore always see humans as creatures that have the ability to choose goals for themselves as well as the ability to plan and execute these goals (i.e., rational nature).

All persons, as a part of rational nature, have a kind of dignity that everyone is bound to respect. For Kant, this respect is epitomized in the "kingdom of ends." The *kingdom of ends* exemplifies for Kant what a free and well-ordered society would be like. Kant tells us that in the *kingdom of ends* ". . . each person remains at liberty to seek his happiness in any way he thinks best so long as he does not violate that universal freedom under the law and, consequently, the rights of other fellow subjects."[36] The *kingdom of ends* therefore holds the promise that respect for the dignity of all individuals can be reconciled with a stable and well-ordered society.

The trouble, however, is that Kant's notion of the *kingdom of ends* appears to leave us with a similar difficulty as that encountered with Rousseau's *general will*—it appears to force individuals to be free. This is especially apparent when Kant writes:

> [The *kingdom of ends*] is the limitation of each person's freedom so that it is compatible with the freedom of everyone, insofar as this is possible in accord with a universal law. . . . Now since every limitation of freedom by the will of another is called coercion, it follows that the civil constitution is a relation among *free* men . . . who yet stand under coercive laws, for reason itself . . . wills it so.[37]

This difficulty brings us to the third part of Kant's moral theory, his principle of autonomy:

> [E]very rational being as an end in himself must be able to regard himself with reference to all laws to which he may be subject as being at the same time the legislator of universal law, for just this very fitness of his maxims for the legislation of universal law distinguishes him as an end in himself.[38]

In other words, acting in accordance with the moral law is not acting in accordance with an external standard (i.e., heteronomy), but acting in accordance with a law that we legislate to ourselves (i.e., autonomy). This view forms the heart of Kant's third formulation of the categorical imperative: ". . . every rational being must so act as if he were through his maxim always a legislating member in the universal kingdom of ends."[39] This explains why the coercion required by the *kingdom of ends* is not a heteronymous restriction on individual freedom—as had appeared to be the case with Rousseau—but an expression of that freedom. Individual freedom is expressed when one acts in accordance with reason because doing otherwise, out of passion or desire for example, would be to act out of control. In other words, true freedom is found when our reason can overcome or control our passions and desires, while succumbing to passion and desire is the worst form of slavery.

This brief excursion into Kant's moral theory provides us with the basic outline of Kant's notion of autonomy. In order to see its relevance to his political philosophy however it is important to also look at Kant's notion of enlightenment. This notion is found in his essay "What is Enlightenment?" where he puts forth the view that immaturity—to be ruled in a manner analogous to the way that a parent controls their child—is ". . . the worst *despotism* we can think of . . ."[40] For Kant, the virtue of enlightenment's commitment to rationality is the kind of self-reliant independence it provides. As he writes:

> *Enlightenment is man's emergence from his self-imposed immaturity. Immaturity* is the inability to use one's understanding without guidance from another. This immaturity is *self-imposed* when its cause lies not in lack of understanding, but in lack of resolve and courage to use it without guidance from another.[41]

For Kant, reason, freedom, and moral accountability are therefore all intimately related to each other. For example, if a person is not free (i.e., cannot act otherwise), then that person cannot be held morally accountable, since an "ought" implies "can." On Hume's account, people are driven to act solely by heteronymous impulses (e.g., sentiments and tradition), so the role of reason is reduced on Hume's account to mere calculation. This, Kant believes, would make morality and justice impossible. For Kant, morality and justice are only possible if individuals are free to act in accordance with principles of the right (i.e., reason) and not always driven to action by heteronymous impulses (e.g., emotions or habit). Therefore, in order for morality and justice to be possible it is necessary, pace Hume, that persons be both rational and free.

With this account of moral autonomy firmly in place, I now return to the issue of political legitimacy and in particular the question of why and when a political regime's authority ought to be respected? The general answer that social contract theory has given to this question is that subjects are bound to respect a regime's authority when they have consented to it and doing so would offer an improvement over, or at least not a worsening of, the conditions found in the state of nature. Yet, as we saw in Hume's objection, this answer might entail either a dangerous fiction or vicious circular reasoning. Kant's response to Hume is to remind him that the social contract is ". . . a *mere idea* of reason, [but] one, however, that has indubitable (practical) reality."[42] In other words, the social contract is a heuristic device, similar to the categorical imperative, whose function is to reveal to us our political rights and duties. This means that even if Hume is correct—that there never was nor would be an original social contract—we can still think of the social contract and the obligations entailed from it as dictates of reason. If this is the case, then we have a self-imposed duty to fulfill these obligations. If we do not fulfill these obligations, then we are both acting against our own freedom and are accountable for failing to do so.

Apart from responding to Hume's objection, Kant's account of autonomy also provides us with a way out of the *liberty dilemma*. Recall here that freedom in Rousseau's *general will* consisted of mastery over oneself because as Rousseau stated ". . . to be driven by appetite alone is slavery, and obedience to the law one has prescribed for oneself is liberty."[43] In his *kingdom of ends*, Kant mirrors Rousseau's sentiments so he is able to avoid the first horn of the *liberty dilemma*. The *kingdom of ends* provides us with a positive notion of liberty that promotes engaged citizenship and embraces the political values of democratic self-determination and universal equality.

Yet, as we saw at the end of the Rousseau section, Rousseau was able to overcome the first horn of the *liberty dilemma* only by appealing to a kind of the collectivism that then left his account vulnerable to the second horn of the *liberty dilemma*: too much government infringement can undermine the negative liberty of individuals. This difficulty, however, is overcome in Kant's notion of autonomy. Unlike Rousseau, Kant makes specific references to the importance of the individual, specifically the idea that an individual should strive to obtain maturity and that as part of rational nature they have a dignity that ought not be transgressed. This recovery of the individual by Kant makes his account less susceptible to the charge of collectivism and therefore allows Kant to avoid the second horn of the *liberty dilemma* as well.

Kant's account of autonomy thereby provides an attractive way out of the *liberty dilemma* and also a solid response to the conservative objection of Hume. It is not, however, without its problems. The next two sections will outline two objections against Kant's account of autonomy. The first is a descriptive objection that comes from the utilitarian tradition. This objection is a recovery of Hume's position, arguing that liberty is actually more closely aligned to utility (i.e., to a notion of the good) than with a notion of the right (i.e., reason). This objection rests on the view that human flourishing is closely tied to the attainment of pleasure and the avoidance of pain.

The second is a normative objection that comes from the Marxist tradition. This objection accepts Kant's civic-republican notion of human flourishing (i.e., humans have intrinsic dignity and are by nature political animals), but argues that by living in an irrational society (e.g., capitalism) people become irrational (e.g., susceptible to false consciousness). This means that in order to be free (i.e., to act in accordance with reason) society must first be made rational (e.g., become communist) so that it no longer deforms individuals.

THE UTILITARIAN OBJECTION TO KANT'S ACCOUNT OF AUTONOMY

The utilitarian objection to Kant's notion of autonomy arises out of Hume's skepticism toward most moral and political principles. As already mentioned, this skepticism stemmed from Hume's descriptive account of humans as fundamentally creatures of habit. For Hume, this meant humans were moved to act from emotion and custom rather than reason. Kant's account of autonomy, while persuasive, never actually disproved Hume's descriptive claim. Kant instead offered a normative, and not descriptive, response to Hume. Kant argued that if morality and justice were possible, then it would be necessary for persons to be rational and free. But even if this is true, it does not actually prove that humans are in fact motivated by, or could be made to act in accordance with, reason. The utilitarian objection to Kant begins here.

Utilitarianism is a school of thought that is very suspicious of rights-based discourse—specifically universal rights. For example, the founder of utilitarianism, Jeremy Bentham, is famous for having said that: "Natural rights is simple nonsense: natural and imprescriptible rights, rhetorical nonsense—nonsense upon stilts."[44] This puts the utilitarian tradition very much at odds with the social contract tradition, which exclusively works within a rights-based discourse. The utilitarian tradition instead takes utility as its first and most basic principle. This principle is understood as maximizing pleasure or interest and minimizing pain or cost.[45] John Stuart Mill articulates the difference between the two and highlights the strength of the utilitarian position when he claims to forgo:

> . . . any advantage which could be derived to my argument from the idea of abstract right as a thing independent of utility. I regard utility as the ultimate appeal on all ethical questions; but it must be utility in the largest sense, grounded on the permanent interests of man as a progressive being.[46]

In this quote, Mill is making two important points. First, he is not simply dismissing the notion of rights. Rights, for Mill, are important and something that ought to be protected, but only to the degree that they are based on and help to promote utility. As Mill rhetorically states: "If the objector goes on to ask, why [rights are valuable]? I can give him no other reason than general utility."[47] Second, not just any type of utility ought to be promoted, but utility which, as Mill puts it, advances ". . . the permanent interests of man as a progressive being."

To understand this last phrasing of utility, we need to mention that utilitarianism, as Mill acknowledges, has always been susceptible to the criticism that it is ". . . utterly mean and groveling, as a doctrine worthy only of swine. . . ."[48] Mill's response to this objection is to make the concession that not all pleasures are equal. Some pleasures, he argues, are higher and others are lower. The higher pleasures ought to be preferred over the lower because the higher ones promote the betterment of humankind. Obtaining the higher pleasures make us better people and that betterment translates to more utility. This ranking of pleasures might appear to move Mill away from traditional utilitarianism, but as he argues:

It is quite compatible with the principle of utility to recognize the fact that some kinds of pleasure are more desirable and more valuable than others. It would be absurd that, while in estimating all other things quality is considered as well as quantity, the estimation of pleasure should be supposed to depend on quantity alone.[49]

While this is a very rough outline of utilitarianism, and in particular Mill's version of it, it is sufficient to provide enough of a context to understand the utilitarian response to the liberty concern. This response is best articulated by Mill, in *On Liberty*, when he states that:

the sole end for which mankind are warranted, individually or collectively, in interfering with the liberty of action of any of their number, is self-protection. That the only purpose for which power can be rightfully exercised over any member of a civilized community, against his will, is to prevent harm to others. His own good, either physical or moral, is not a sufficient warrant.[50]

This principle has come to be known as the "harm principle" because of its obvious implication: anything is permissible, including harm to oneself, so long as it harms no one else.

For Mill, the *harm principle* is primarily aimed at protecting the opinions of minorities from the tyranny of the majority. On this account, no point of view, so long as it does not violate the *harm principle*, can or should be shut out of a democratic society. This is because the more diversity of views there are on an issue, the more such discussion will tend to lead to a better understanding of it. If a particular view were to be shut out of the discussion, Mill tells us it would be problematic for two complementary reasons. "If the opinion is right, [we] are deprived of the opportunity of exchanging error for truth: if wrong, [we] lose, what is almost as great a benefit, the clearer perception and livelier impression of truth, produced by its collision with error."[51] Mill thought that since democracies would only continue to grow in number, it was imperative that societies be on guard against the suppression of minority opinions.[52]

The potential threat to liberty that Mill identified here is diametrically opposed to the threat identified in Rousseau's civic-republicanism. For Rousseau, the threat to liberty came not from the potential tyranny of the majority, but from the tyranny of a minority (e.g., the elite) who imposed their will on the majority either through force or fraud. In this sense, the utilitarian notion of liberty offers a return back to the classical liberal notion of negative liberty.

The upside of the utilitarian account is its ability to both defend a notion of liberty and still take seriously Hume's descriptive account that emotion and habit, not reason, is what ultimately motivates people to act. The utilitarian conclusion therefore can be summarized as follows: even if what initially motivates us to action are our sentiments (i.e., our desire for pleasure or avoidance of pain), we are still free so long as our actions do not harm others and are rational in so far as we use our reason in determine the greatest good. By undercutting the Kantian notion of dignity and replacing it with utility, utilitarianism undermines Kant's resolution of the *liberty dilemma*. On the utilitarian account, democratic self-determination, individual freedom and universal equality can all cohere with each other, but only so long as they work together to promote the greater good.

THE MARXIST OBJECTION TO KANT'S ACCOUNT OF AUTONOMY

A second challenge to Kant's account of autonomy is found in the work of Karl Marx. Marx, unlike the utilitarians, is not concerned with maximizing utility, but with combating exploitation and alienation. In this regard, Marx's view of humanity is consistent with the Kantian notion of dignity, especially if we read Marx as demanding that workers be respected as ends in-themselves and not treated as mere means. Marx also appears to have endorsed a positive notion liberty that would have put him squarely within the civic-republican tradition. These observations are evident from the following description Marx provides of what he calls the realm of freedom:

> The realm of freedom really begins only where labour determined by necessity and external expediency ends; it lies by its very nature beyond the sphere of material production proper. Just as the savage must wrestle with nature to satisfy his needs, to maintain and reproduce life, so must civilized man, and he must do so in all forms of society and under all possible modes of production. This realm of natural necessity expands with his development, because his needs do too; but the productive forces to satisfy these expand at the same time. Freedom in this sphere, can consist only in this, that socialized man, the associated producers, govern the human metabolism with nature in a rational way, bringing it under their collective control, instead of being dominated by it as a blind power; accomplishing it with the least expenditure of energy and in conditions most worthy and appropriate for their human nature. But this always remains in the realm of necessity. The true realm of freedom, the development of human powers as an end in itself, begins beyond it, though it can only flourish with this realm of necessity as its basis. The reduction of the working day is the basic prerequisite.[53]

This long passage expresses both Marx's sympathies with and also criticisms of Kant's account of autonomy. Marx and Kant are both in agreement that freedom requires a rational society and that in such a society people should be treated as ends-in-themselves. Marx and Kant differ, however, on what should come first: acting in accordance with reason or establishing a rational society. Recall that for Kant, if we are free, then we ought to be moved to act by principles of right (i.e., reason) and in doing so we are working toward a *kingdom of ends*—a regulative ideal that we might never achieve, but that nonetheless should guide our actions. In short, acting in accordance with reason for Kant is sufficient for obtaining justice.

The critique that the utilitarians (via Hume) leveled against Kant is that people are rarely, if ever, moved to act by reason alone. Instead, utilitarians argued that people are moved to action by pleasures and pains. If correct, this observation raises a difficulty for Kant's notion of autonomy, at least in so far as it might be used to resolve the *liberty dilemma*. Marx's account, however, is able to avoid this difficulty by appealing to Rousseau's communitarian insight that individuals do not exist prior to their community. In other words, individuals are not born with preset values, interests, customs or habits. All of these might come to appear as natural givens, but are in fact the product of the society people are born into and raised. For Marx, it is therefore no surprise that societies based on exploitation and alienation inevitably produce irrational individuals (i.e., individuals who do not act in accordance with reason). If Marx's account is correct and if free individuals (i.e., people who act in accordance with reason) are the end goal of any moral or political system, then a rational society (i.e., a society of nondomination) must first be established. This is a slight but nonetheless significant inversion of the Kantian account.

In many ways Marx's account is just an extension of Rousseau's insight that class society perpetuates unjust inequalities, which in turn restrain the freedom of individuals. Marx believed that if the history of economic development were taken seriously, it would be clear that current class inequalities are the product of an irrational social order, and it is this order that must be changed if there are to be individuals who act in accordance with reason. Marx believed that this would be possible only through the emancipation of the working class.

According to Marx, capitalist societies not only prevent individuals from being rational and acting freely, which on Kant's view are violations of their human dignity, but also contain two key contradictions. These contradictions, according to Marx, manifest themselves in two different types of crises: overproduction and the tendency of the rate of profit to fall. Both of these contradictions lead to inevitable economic crises, which have a similar appearance and effect to natural disasters. Marx argued that these inherent crises would ultimately resolve themselves in one of two ways: "either in a revolutionary reconstruction of society at large, or in the common ruin of the contending classes."[54] In other words, capitalism, by its nature, is an un-free, irrational, and self-destructive system.

Marx therefore contributes two important insights to this discussion. First, he reiterates Rousseau's point that in order to develop a stable and well-ordered society (i.e., address the security concern), the issue of class inequality needs to be resolved and not merely dismissed as an unchangeable fact of reality. Addressing the issue of class inequality, however, requires the development of a rational system of production (e.g., democratic control of the means of production), which brings us to the second insight. For Marx, individuals can only start to become autonomous in the Kantian sense when class society is finally overthrown and a truly free and rational society (i.e., communism) takes its place. This is because in a class society individuals are often rewarded and encouraged to act irrationally (e.g., take big risks). For this reason, it is important to understand, empirically and not just *a priori*, how class societies function and why they are exploitive and alienating (i.e., irrational). When the true nature of class society is understood, then it will also become apparent how and why the interest of the working class—much like Rousseau's *general will*—represents the universal interest.

While these very brief accounts of utilitarianism and Marxism are far from exhaustive, they are sufficient to show the tensions in Kant's responses to the liberty concern. In a classical liberal sense, utilitarians argued that the interests of the collective would be best and most efficiently met when individuals were allowed to freely pursue their own best interest. In contrast, Marxism argued that only by pursuing a more universal interest (e.g., the interest of the working class) would self-determination and universal equality finally be possible. The next section provides an outline of John Rawls's response to these shortcomings in the Kantian account and perhaps also the most viable resolution of the *liberty dilemma*.

RAWLS'S JUSTICE AS FAIRNESS

Given the account of moral and political philosophy thus far provided in Chapters 1 and 2, John Rawls's groundbreaking *A Theory of Justice* can be read as an attempt to accomplish four principle tasks: (1) recognize the Hobbesian insight that with regard to the security concern it is rational for people to hedge their bets; (2) continue the Kantian project of championing the social contract tradition while also keeping Hume's criticisms squarely in mind; (3) respond to the utilitarian objection that a well-ordered society should be based on principles of the good rather than principles of the right and; (4) present a brand of liberalism that can take seriously Rousseau and Marx's insight about inequality being both unjust (e.g., a source of domination) and social destabilizing (i.e., a source of insecurity).

Much like Kant before him, Rawls saw his task as an attempt to salvage the redeemable qualities of the social contract tradition. For Rawls, one of the redeemable aspects of this tradition was its underlying commitment to fairness. In the social contract tradition, principles of justice were discovered by imagining an original agreement that everyone would ideally find acceptable.[55] Rawls found that undergirding this original agreement was a spirit of fairness that could be retained if instead of beginning from some mythical state of nature, political theory began from a less metaphysically laden "original position." The original position suggested by Rawls is a lot like the state of nature, in that it is a thought experiment that tries to mimic the conditions of setting up rules to a game before the game begins. A lot like Kant's categorical imperative, the original position attempts to determine universal principles grounded in reason, as opposed to developing ad hoc rules based on consequences.

Rawls's original position is an imagined scenario where a rational person goes behind a "veil of ignorance." The function of the veil is to act like a filter, leaving the person behind the veil with knowledge only of general facts but no specific facts. For example, under the veil of ignorance one might know about the Great Depression and the destructive impact that economic crises can have on both society and individuals, but they would not know if they themselves would be wealthy or poor, in good health or bad, young or old in that society. Rawls also stipulated that those who went behind the veil of ignorance must assume that the principles decided upon in the original position would apply to a closed society or as he put it, a society ". . . we enter only by birth and exit only by death."[56] This assumption was meant to generate a kind of buy-in from those behind the veil and to stress the intergenerational aspect of justice.

Following Hobbes's risk aversion strategy, Rawls believed that when put in the original position the most rational course of action for one to pursue would be for one to hedge their bets. From behind a veil of ignorance, Rawls surmised that a rational person would derive the kinds of principles that would aim to prevent or ameliorate disastrous situations, such as totalitarian forms of government or severe economic crises. Rawls therefore concluded that in the original position rational persons would converge on two fundamental principles of justice.[57] The first would be that all persons should be entitled to the same basic set of liberties. In Rawls's own words: "each person is to have an equal right to the most extensive scheme of equal basic liberties compatible with a similar scheme of liberties for others."[58] These basic liberties would be non-negotiable, meaning they cannot be taken away, either by a private entity, government, or democratic vote, and they also could not be traded away by those who possess them. As Rawls states: "Each person possess an inviolability founded on justice that even the welfare of society as a whole cannot override. For this reason justice denies that the loss of freedom for some is made right by a greater good shared by others."[59]

Rawls' first principle can be seen as responding to both the worry expressed above over Rousseau's *general will* and the utilitarian tradition as a whole.[60] It also has very clear ties to Locke's understanding of individual freedom and Kant's notion of dignity (i.e., treating others not merely as a means). Rawls believed that no one in the original position would consent to a society whose basic structure would put the interest or will of the majority ahead of the dignity or rights of individuals. This principle is commonly referred to as the "liberty principle" and it gets us half way to resolving the *liberty dilemma* by safeguarding individual freedom and thereby avoiding the first horn of the *liberty dilemma*. It also avoids leaving us in a *security dilemma* by denying regimes the possibility of striping individuals of their moral or political standing in society, thereby avoiding the state of exception horn of the *security dilemma* as well.

Rawls's second principle, known as the "difference principle," addresses the issue of inequality. For Rawls, the problem of inequality is not so much that there are inequalities, but that too much inequality of a certain kind can be oppressive and destabilizing to a society. The task of justice is therefore to determine at what point inequality begins to negatively impacts people's life chances and what principle could be put in place to help to ameliorate or prevent this.

Working from the original position, Rawls believed that one would have to take seriously the possibility that s/he might find themselves at the bottom of the social hierarchy. In this regard, Rawls again adopted a kind of Hobbesian risk-averse approach: assume the worst possible scenario in order to find principles of justice. If the possibility of being the worstoff were taken seriously, Rawls believed that rational beings would again hedge their bets and arrive at something like the following conclusion: "Social and economic inequalities are to be arranged so that they are both (a) reasonably expected to be to everyone's advantage, and (b) attached to positions and offices open to all."[61]

Another way of putting this is to say that whatever inequalities exist within society, a just basic structure would make sure that inequalities are set up in such a way that they benefit those who are in the worst position. While this might at first appear to be a justification of inequality, it is in fact a shifting of the burden of proof. The difference principle makes it so that all inequalities must be assumed unjust unless they can be shown to make the worstoff better off.

As we can see from this second principle, Rawls's political view is not as radical as those expressed by Rousseau or Marx, but it does share with them the common concern that too much inequality undermines democratic self-determination, individual freedom, and also security. In addressing these issues, Rawls's second principle therefore completes the task of resolving the *liberty dilemma* and does so without reintroducing a *security dilemma*.

It addresses the Hobbesian worry of an ever-present threat of a state of nature by providing principles for a stable and well-ordered society, while also recovering the positive notion of liberty championed by the civic-republican tradition.

CONCLUSION

This chapter has provided an exploration into the *liberty dilemma*: the problem of trying to reconcile commitments to democratic self-determination, individual freedom and universal equality. Classical liberalism has traditionally represented the first horn of this dilemma in prioritizing individual freedom over universal equality and democratic self-determination. Civic-republicanism, in prioritizing democratic self-determination and universal equality over individual freedom, has represented the other horn of this dilemma. Resolving this dilemma is important because, as we saw in Chapter 1, the Philadelphia model of sovereignty—the resolution I proposed to the *security dilemma*—depends on there being a consistent way to address the liberty concern.

In this chapter, I suggested that Immanuel Kant's account of autonomy ultimately provides the correct blueprint for overcoming the *liberty dilemma*. Kant's account, however, was not without its critics. Utilitarians critiqued Kant for not sufficiently understanding that our actions are primarily motivated by our desire for pleasure and aversion to pain, and that this, not the abstract dictates of reason, is what ultimately undergirds any notion of rights. Marxists in turn critiqued Kant for not appreciating enough how irrational societies (e.g., a capitalist society) can produce irrational persons (e.g., alienated and exploited workers) who cannot in turn act in accordance with reason. John Rawls two principles of justice, however, appear to have addressed those criticisms and thereby maintained the core of Kant's resolution to the *liberty dilemma*.

In this regard, Rawls's accomplishment cannot be understated. His position, however, is also not without its own problems. For our purposes, the most pressing concern stems from Rawls restricting his theory of justice to the domestic sphere and having little to say (at least initially) about what global or international justice demands.[62] So while Rawls's framework might be able to resolve the *liberty dilemma* at the domestic level, it is not clear what kind of guidance it can provide internationally for cases that involve the liberty, security, and equality of foreigners (e.g., immigration). In large part this is because in developing his original position Rawls assumed a closed society. As mentioned above, this assumption was necessary in order to generate buy-in and to account for justice between generations. As we will see more clearly in the next chapter, this assumption makes Rawls' resolution of the *liberty dilemma* less complete than initially thought.

NOTES

1. John Locke, *Second Treaties of Government*, ed. C.B. Macpherson (Indianapolis: Hackett Publishing, 1980), 48–50.

2. Ibid., 8–16.

3. Ibid., 72.

4. Thomas Hobbes, *Leviathan*, ed. Edwin Curley (Indianapolis: Hackett Publishing, 1994), 110–111.

5. See Locke, *Second Treaties of Government*, 77–78.

6. Ibid., 107–124.

7. Ibid., 66.

8. Ibid., 18–30.

9. Isaiah Berlin, "Two Concepts of Liberty," in *Four Essays on Liberty* (London: Oxford University Press, 2002), 121.

10. Jean-Jacques Rousseau, "On the Social Contract," in *The Basic Political Writings*, trans. Donald Cress (Indianapolis: Hackett Publishing, 1987), 141.

11. Jean-Jacques Rousseau, "Discourse on the Origin of Inequality," in *The Basic Political Writings*, trans. Donald Cress (Indianapolis: Hackett Publishing, 1987) 58.

12. I share a similar reading of Rousseau with Charles Mills, who extends this reading to issues concerning race and the social contract. See Charles Mills, "The Domination Contract," in *Contract and Domination*, Carole Pateman and Charles Mills (Malden, MA: Polity Press, 2007) 79–105.

13. Locke, *Second Treaties of Government*, 63–65.

14. Rousseau, "Discourse on the Origin of Inequality," 70.

15. Ibid., 64.

16. Ibid., 65.

17. Ibid., 80.

18. Rousseau, "On the Social Contract," 141.

19. Ibid., 151.

20. Ibid.,150.

21. Ibid.,170–171.

22. David Hume, "Of Parties in General," *Political Writings*, ed. Stuart D. Warner and Donald W. Livingston (Indianapolis: Hackett Publishing Company, 1994), 161.

23. David Hume, "Of the Original Contract." *Political Writings*, ed. Stuart D. Warner and Donald W. Livingston (Indianapolis: Hackett Publishing Company, 1994), 164.

24. Ibid.,168.

25. Ibid.,168.

26. David Hume, "Of the Origin of Justice and Property," *Political Writings*, ed. Stuart D. Warner and Donald W. Livingston (Indianapolis: Hackett Publishing Company, 1994), 15.

27. Ibid., 7–8.

28. Ibid.,17.

29. Ibid., 11.

30. Hume, "Of the Original Contract," 171–172.

31. Ibid.,180–181.

32. Immanuel Kant, "Grounding for the Metaphysics of Morals," *Ethical Philosophy*, trans. James Ellington (Indianapolis: Hackett Publishing Company, 1983), 2.

33. David Hume, *An Enquiry Concerning The Principles of Morals*, ed. J.B. Schneewind (Indianapolis: Hackett Publishing Company, 1983) 83.

34. Kant, "Grounding for the Metaphysics Of Morals," 30.

35. Ibid., 36.

36. Kant, "On the Proverb: That May be True in Theory, But Is of No Practical Use," *Perpetual Peace and Other Essays*. Trans. Ted Humphrey. (Indianapolis/Cambridge: Hackett Publishing Company, 1983), 73.

37. Ibid., 72.

38. Kant, "Grounding For The Metaphysics Of Morals," 43.

39. Ibid., 43.

40. Kant, "On the Proverb: That May be True in Theory, But Is of No Practical Use," 73.

41. Immanuel Kant, "An Answer to the Question: What is Enlightenment?," in *Perpetual Peace and Other Essays*, trans. Ted Humphrey (Indianapolis/ Cambridge: Hackett Publishing Company, 1983), 41.

42. Kant, "On the Proverb: That May be True in Theory, But Is of No Practical Use," 77.

43. See Chapter 2, 59.

44. Jeremy Bentham, "Anarchical Fallacies; Being an Examination of the Declarations of Rights Issued During the French Revolution—an Examination of the Rights of Man and the Citizen Decreed by the Constituent Assembly in France," in *The Works of Jeremy Bentham Vol 2*, ed. John Bowring (London: Elibron Classics, 2005), 501.

45. John Stuart Mill, *Utilitarianism*, ed. George Sher (Indianapolis: Hackett Publishing Company, 2001), 6.

46. John Stuart Mill, *On Liberty*, ed. Elizabeth Rapaport (Indianapolis: Hackett Publishing Company, 1978), 10.

47. Mill, *Utilitarianism*, 54.

48. Mill, *Utilitarianism*, 7.

49. Ibid., 8.

50. Mill, *On Liberty*, 9.

51. Ibid., 16.

52. Ibid., 3–4.

53. Karl Marx, *Capital Vol 3: A Critique of Political Economy*, trans. David Fernbach (London: Penguin Classics, 1991), 958–959.

54. Karl Marx, and Frederick Engels, *The Communist Manifesto*, trans. Samuel Moore, ed. David McLellan (Oxford/New York: Oxford University Press, 1998), 3.

55. John Rawls, *A Theory of Justice*, (Cambridge, MA: Harvard University Press, 1971), 10.

56. John Rawls, *Justice As Fairness: A Restatement*, ed. Erin Kelly (Cambridge, MA: Harvard University Press, 2001), 40.

57. Rawls, *A Theory of Justice*, 14–15.

58. Ibid., 53.

59. Ibid., 3–4.

60. Henry Sidgwick, *The Methods of Ethics*, (Chicago: University of Chicago Press, 1962).

61. Rawls, *A Theory of Justice*, 53.

62. See Charles R. Beitz, "Justice and International Relations." *Philosophy & Public Affairs* 4.4 (1975): 360–389.

Chapter 3

The Immigration Debate within Philosophy

In Chapter 1, I introduced the *security dilemma* suggesting that the current immigration policies of places like the US are in such a dilemma: trying to avoid falling into a Hobbesian state of nature but in doing so fostering the conditions that give rise to an Agambenian state of exception. At the end of that chapter, I proposed a way of resolving the dilemma by appealing to a concept of sovereignty that gives priority to the liberty concern (i.e., a constitutional democracy) instead of one that gives priority to the security concern (i.e., totalitarianism). That proposal appeared promising, but in Chapter 2 we saw that this concept of sovereignty also runs into its own internal difficulty: the *liberty dilemma*. This dilemma arises from the fact that constitutional democracies (e.g., a Philadelphia model of sovereignty) require a commitment to democratic self-determination, individual freedom, and universal equality, but reconciling these three commitments can be difficult since they are based on conflicting notions of liberty: positive and negative liberty.

In Chapter 2, I went on to make the case that Kant's account of autonomy ultimately provides the blueprint for resolving the *liberty dilemma*, but his account was not perfect. It received strong criticism from both the utilitarian and Marxist traditions. In response to this criticism, I suggested that Rawls's theory of justice supplements Kant's account and provides it with an adequate response to both its utilitarian and Marxist critics. The Rawlsian account therefore appeared to finally resolve the *liberty dilemma*, but as mentioned at the conclusion of the last chapter, this resolution depended on a key assumption. It assumed that everyone subject to the coercive power of government entered the political community only by birth and exited only by death. When considering justice at the global or international level—especially with respect to an issue like immigration—this key assumption does not hold up and this throws us back into a *liberty dilemma*.

This chapter will examine why this is the case and how the issue of immigration best exemplifies the *liberty dilemma* at a more global level. We will see that on the one hand some philosophers believe that too much individual freedom (i.e., freedom of movement) can undermine both democratic self-determination and political equality (e.g., partiality to co-nationals). On the other hand, we will see that other philosophers believe that too strong of an emphasis on democratic self-determination and partiality to co-nationals undermines commitments to both individual freedom and universal equality (i.e., giving noncitizens equal moral consideration).

This chapter therefore provides a summary of the early philosophical debate over immigration, arguing that this debate is best understood as a recasting of the *liberty dilemma* at the global scale. The breakdown of the chapter is therefore as follows. The first section introduces the two opposing poles of the philosophical debate over immigration. On one side are those who believe that a political community has a presumptive right to exclude foreigners, while the other side makes a case for open-borders. The second section looks at two competing attempts to reconcile the two sides. The first is the liberal-nationalist position, which attempts to return the discussion of immigration back to its contractarian roots. The other is the liberal cosmopolitan account, which concludes that notions of sovereignty and citizenship need to be rethought as multi-layered concepts. The conclusion of this chapter is that with regard to the issue of immigration, the *liberty dilemma* returns in a new globalized form and that resolving this dilemma ought to the primary concern of moral and political philosophers.

THE ETHICS OF IMMIGRATION

The current philosophical work on immigration can trace its starting point back to Michael Walzer's *Spheres of Justice.* In that book, Walzer attempted to provide a communitarian response to John Rawls. In his criticism of Rawls, Walzer highlighted an important difference between liberal and communitarian approaches to justice. Classical liberals, as we saw in the previous chapter, have assumed that the individual is prior to his/her community, which means that such things as individual rights have moral and political priority. Communitarians, on the other hand, believe that the community is prior to the individual and that notions such as individual rights only have meaning if the community is given priority. On this view, understanding justice requires first getting clear about who or what the community is. Therefore, at the heart of Walzer's criticism of Rawls is the question of political membership: who gets to count as part of the political community, why, and by whom?

On Rawls's account, the question of membership did not play much of a role. As already mentioned, Rawls proceeds as though that question is settled prior to entering the original position, but for Walzer (and other communitarians) the settling of this question is one of the most fundamental parts of understanding justice. As Walzer writes:

> The primary good that we distribute to one another is membership in some human community. And what we do with regard to membership structures all our other distributive choices: it determines with whom we make those choices, from whom we require obedience and collect taxes, to whom we allocate goods and services[1] [furthermore] . . . it is only as members somewhere that men and women can hope to share in all the other social goods—security, wealth, honor, office, and power—that communal life makes possible.[2]

By assuming an already established and closed off political community, Walzer believes that Rawls basically took for granted one of the most important questions of justice.

On Walzer's view, the ability to confer political membership on individuals ". . . is both a matter of political choice and moral constraint."[3] By political choice, Walzer means that political communities, much like clubs, have a vital interest in shaping their collective character. This interest is so fundamental that, with only a few exceptions,[4] political communities have a presumptive right to admit or exclude foreigners as they see fit. Once a foreigner is admitted, however, Walzer believes that a political community is morally obligated to extend to them full membership rights. As he notes: "Naturalization . . . is entirely constrained: every new immigrant, every refugee taken in, every resident and worker must be offered the opportunities of citizenship."[5] Walzer's position is therefore buoyed by a strong civic-republican commitment to democratic self-determination and political equality. Political communities are self-determined in that they are free to exclude foreigners, but politically equal in that every person within the political community (including recently admitted foreigners) must have access to full membership status. Walzer therefore summarizes his view on immigration in the following way: "Across a considerable range of the decisions that are made, states are simply free to take strangers in (or not)."[6]

In "Aliens and Citizens: The Case for Open Borders," Joseph Carens provides a counter-argument to Walzer's view. In that essay, Carens begins by pointing out how, in a world like ours, restrictions on migration help to maintain unjust global conditions. According to Carens, membership in political communities today is a lot like feudal privileges of the past, where most people did nothing either to deserve or be burdened with the kind of status they happen to hold and there is little one can do to change it. Similarly, most people today acquire citizenship either by their place of birth or through ancestry—usually inheriting the citizenship of one or both of their parents. So while most people have citizenship in at least one country, not all forms of citizenship are equal. For example, being a citizen of a country in the Global North comes with a greater set of opportunities than being a citizen of a country in the Global South. On its face, this arbitrary and disproportionate distribution of opportunities seems unfair and unjust (i.e., a violation of universal equality). So assuming that the foreign migrants in question are not criminals, subversives, or armed invaders, Carens asks what politically or morally can justify using coercive force to prevent individuals from upgrading the membership status into which they were born?

The rest of Carens's essay challenges the idea that political communities ought to have a presumptive right to exclude foreigners and makes the case that borders should be (fairly) open. Carens's argument in defense of (fairly) open-borders is two-pronged. First, it goes through three traditional liberal positions and shows how each of them cannot defend a political community's presumptive right to exclude foreigners. It then looks at Walzer's communitarian position and offers some persuasive reasons for why his position too fails to offer conclusive support for political communities having a presumptive right to exclude foreigners.

Carens argument begins by looking at the libertarian (i.e., classical liberal) position, specifically the one put forth by Robert Nozick in *State, Anarchy and Utopia*. According to Carens, the kind of minimal state advocated by Nozick and presumably other libertarians,". . . has no right to do anything other than enforce the rights which individuals already enjoy in the state of nature."[7] With this in mind, Carens asks us to imagine a case where a US farmer wants to hire a Mexican worker and where the Mexican worker wants to work for the US farmer. Carens concludes that on Nozick's account, a government that restricts the movement of the Mexican worker would be violating the rights of both these individuals. It would violate the US farmer's right to hire the Mexican worker and the Mexican worker's right to sell his labor to the US farmer.[8] While this example might not undermine all arguments against open-borders, it is sufficient to show that the libertarian account has a very difficult, if not impossible, task of trying to justify immigration exclusions. It ". . . provides no basis for the state to exclude aliens and no basis for individuals to exclude aliens that could not also be used to exclude citizens as well."[9]

Carens then considers the possibility of justifying exclusions under a Rawlsian (i.e., liberal egalitarian) framework. Carens acknowledges that Rawls's framework is based on a closed society, but asks what his framework would entail if it were applied at a global level. After all, Carens points out:

> many of the reasons that make the original position useful in thinking about questions of justice within a given society also make it useful for thinking about justice across different societies . . . anyone who wants to be moral will feel obligated to justify the use of force against other human beings, whether they are members of the same society or not.[10]

From there, Carens goes on to argue that under a global original position international political communities would also be constrained by principles of justice, meaning they could not restrict freedoms such as religious freedom and all inequalities among political communities would be restricted by something like an international difference principle.[11] So whether any sort of immigration restrictions are justified on this account would rest on whether freedom of movement is or is not considered a basic liberty at the global level. Carens believes that it should be. After all, if the right to free movement is important within a political community, then it stands to reason that it should be important between political communities as well.[12] But even if global freedom of movement is not necessarily a basic liberty and thereby protected by Rawls's liberty principle, it does seem as though immigration restrictions tend to harm those who globally speaking are the least well off by trapping them and not allowing them to better their situation through migration. If this is the case, then a difference principle at the global level would seem to support the idea of a world without borders. In either case, it would be difficult to justify immigration restrictions from a Rawlsian position.

Finally, Carens considers the utilitarian view with respect to immigration restrictions. As we saw in the previous chapter, at the heart of any utilitarian approach is the maximization of utility and a commitment to making sure everyone's interests are taken into consideration. On this account, Carens concludes that it would be ". . . hard to believe that a utilitarian calculus which took the interests of aliens seriously would justify . . . limits on immigration."[13] The reason being that, regardless of the costs increased immigration might have (although there are strong reasons to believe that increased immigration would actually be a net gain for all), the benefits it would bring to the globally worst off will easily outweigh any presumed costs to those who are globally better off.

This brings the first part of Carens's argument to a close. This part of the argument seems to show that from any given liberal perspective (e.g., libertarian, egalitarian, or utilitarian) restrictions on migration are difficult, if not impossible, to justify. Yet even if Carens is right about liberal theory, his arguments seem to do little to undermine Walzer's argument. Walzer, after all, did not offer a strictly liberal but instead a communitarian justification for immigration restrictions. Carens recognizes this point and so moves on to consider Walzer's communitarian position in the second half of this chapter.

Carens criticizes Walzer's position by challenging two of the principle reasons Walzer provides in defense of immigration restrictions. First, Walzer claims that a sense of distinctiveness is necessary for a political community to exist and this sense of distinctiveness would be put at risk if the borders between political communities were opened. In other words, a sense of distinctiveness is not possible without political communities being at some level closed off.[14] For example, if France were to suddenly open it borders, it could soon be overrun by non-French immigrants and quickly lose its French distinctiveness, which not only gives France its unique character but also its social cohesiveness.

Carens objects to this by pointing out that: "What makes for distinctiveness and what erodes it is much more complex than political control of admissions."[15] As examples, Carens cites various cities, provinces, and states that can and do remain distinctive, even though they have little to no control over admissions. For example, the state of California is able to remain distinct from the state of Texas, even though everyone within the US is allowed to migrate freely between them.[16] Therefore a sense of distinctiveness and open-borders are not necessarily antagonistic to each other in the way Walzer believed.

Walzer also defends the right to exclude immigrants by arguing that political communities are analogous to clubs, where a right to freedom of association gives political communities discretion over membership criteria. Carens, however, believes this analogy glosses over an important distinction between public and private. As Carens writes:

> Drawing a line between public and private is often problematic, but it is clear that clubs are normally at one end of the scale and states at the other. So, the fact that private clubs may admit or exclude whomever they choose says nothing about the appropriate admission standards for states.[17]

In glossing over this distinction, Carens believes Walzer failed to address the conflict that arises between freedom of association, which typically wins out in the private sphere, and equal protection, which typically wins out in the public sphere. So without denying that private and intimate associations, like households, should be allowed to have more discretion in determining who it will and will not associate with, it is not clear why public and less intimate associations, like a political community, should enjoy the same amount of discretion. For example, while it might be okay (although not laudable) for an atheist family to exclude religious people from its dinner table, it is not similarly okay for a government institution to hire or not hire people based on religious grounds. In the former case freedom of association wins out, but in the latter case equality of opportunity wins out. Carens believes that the issue of immigration is more like the second case (e.g., public) than the first, so equality of opportunity, not freedom of association, ought to win out. On this point, Carens concludes that:

> No moral argument will seem acceptable to us, if it directly challenges the assumption of the equal moral worth of all individuals. If restrictions on immigration are to be justified, they have to be based on arguments that respect that principle.[18]

The arguments Carens presents against immigration restrictions and in favor of open-borders are very persuasive, but in his essay "Immigration: The Case for Limits" David Miller provides a response to Carens's arguments and concludes that in fact:

> [I]t is possible *both* to argue that every member of the political community, native or immigrant, must be [given equal consideration], *and* to argue that there are good grounds for setting upper bounds both to the rate and the overall number of immigrants who are admitted.[19]

Miller's argument in support of this conclusion begins with an examination of the claim that the right to free movement entails open-borders. Miller concedes that freedom of movement is a basic right, but he suggests that it is not an unlimited right. For example, individuals have a right not to be chained down, but this does not therefore mean that they have an unlimited right to trespass onto other people's private property. Miller agrees that individuals who do not have an adequate range of options where they currently live have a strong interest in migrating elsewhere.[20] But putting extreme cases to the side for a moment, such as religious/political persecution and economic/social displacement (which he later addresses in the third part of his argument), Miller believes that ". . . although people certainly have an *interest* in being able to migrate internationally, they do not have a basic interest of the kind that would be required to ground a human right."[21] At least they do not have a right to immigrate anywhere they want, so long as the political community in which they live already provides them with an adequate range of options.

Next, Miller considers the argument that a right to exit should be symmetrical with a right to enter. According to this argument, if one does not have a right to enter elsewhere then a right to exit (which Miller concedes is a human right) turns out to be not much of a right at all. Miller counters this argument by appealing to a marriage analogy. According to Miller, the right to exit is similar to the right of marriage: ". . . where by no means everyone is able to wed the partner they would ideally like to have, but most have the opportunity to marry *someone*."[22] Miller concedes that if no state offered to take someone in, then the right to exit would indeed have no value, but he argues that this is not the case. According to Miller, states generally are willing to let people in and so long as there is at least one state willing to take that person in, no state has an obligation to take in everyone. This shows that a right to exit does not necessarily entail a right to immigrate, at least not in the sense in which it normally is used.

The final argument Miller considers is the demand for open-borders based on commitments to universal equality. Miller concedes that when states are confronted with people whose lives are less than decent, states ". . . must either ensure that the basic rights of such people are protected in the places where they live—by aid, by intervention, or by some other means—or they must help them move to other communities where their lives will be better."[23] Miller, however, points out that this obligation does not necessitate open-borders, but merely an obligation to work toward improving local conditions. In other words, a commitment to universal equality might obligate a political community to action (e.g., send resources to help struggling foreigners in other countries), but it does not obligate them to take in struggling foreigners.

For Miller, his response to these three arguments show that individuals do not have an unlimited right to move anywhere they like, yet his response does not necessarily entail that political communities therefore have a presumptive right to close off their borders. To establish this further claim, Miller provides two reasons for why political communities should have such a right. First, he argues that a political community has a right to preserve its culture (i.e., cultural continuity which he differentiates from cultural rigidity) such that it would be entitled to have immigration policies that work to ". . . enrich rather than dislocate public culture."[24] Another way of putting this is that liberal democracies require a certain kind of political culture. If too many immigrants with illiberal public cultures are admitted this could threaten democratic liberal governments. Second, overriding concerns, such as the need for population control, could justify giving a state a right to exclude. For example, Miller believes that global overpopulation cannot be addressed until there are restrictions on the movement of people, since he believes that out migration provides a release valve for countries with high birth rates which allows them to maintain those high rates.[25]

In this way, Miller believes he has answered the challenge put forth by Carens. He has shown that restrictions on immigration are not necessarily illiberal and that in fact immigration restrictions might be necessary in order to establish and maintain a liberal democracy. In short, Miller provides some reasons for why commitments to individual freedom and universal equality are not necessarily in conflict with, but might actually depend on, the ability of a political community to control its own border (e.g., democratic self-determination). There are, however, some reasons to be skeptical of Miller's argument. In particular, there is the worry that Miller's argument only reaches this conclusion by distorting the meaning of liberalism.

One such argument against Miller's position can be found in Phillip Cole's *Philosophies of Exclusion*. In that book, Cole defends the claim that ". . . there is a tension, if not an outright contradiction, between the liberal principle of moral equality and the perceived need for closure of liberal polities."[26] Cole believes that this contradiction stems from liberalism's commitment to moral equality and its perceived need to establish and maintain boundaries (i.e., exclude certain persons from equal consideration) in order to make good on liberal commitments to its citizens.

Cole's argument in support of this claim begins with the already familiar premise that liberal theory is committed to a particular set of values: universal equality and autonomy (i.e., democratic self-determination and individual freedom). Cole argues that the first holds that there can be no liberal justification for failing to give anyone, including foreigners, equal moral consideration.[27] The second commitment is expressed in what Cole terms the "rationality principle." This principle is based on the Kantian notion of autonomy which we encountered in the previous chapter: real freedom is giving the moral law to ourselves. As Cole explains:

> [the "rationality principle" begins with] the assumption that all human beings are in principle equally capable of rational thought, and that all political problems are therefore, in principle, capable of a rational solution: appeal to non-rational or arbitrary criteria for solving problems is therefore ruled out.[28]

This principle, as we also saw in Rawls's *Theory of Justice*, has played a prominent role in recent liberal thought. Practices and institutions that negatively affect people's life chances and lack rational justification are deplored as unjust. Cole, in agreement with Walzer, Carens, and Miller, believes that the question of membership is of significant importance in considering issues of justice. Unlike Walzer and Miller (but like Carens), Cole does not see any rational or morally nonarbitrary way of justifying immigration restrictions. On this basis, Cole concludes that: ". . . the only consistently liberal [approach to immigration is] . . . complete freedom of international movement."[29]

Cole defends this conclusion by presenting, what he purports to be, an exhaustive list of the possible approaches that can be taken toward immigration restrictions. The four possibilities are: (1) there is no nonarbitrary membership criteria, so membership restrictions are always in violation of the *rationality principle* and therefore always illiberal; (2) there is no nonarbitrary membership criteria, but the need to establish a political community overrides liberalism's *rationality principle*; (3) there are nonarbitrary membership criteria, but this criterion appeals to notions of "common identity"; and finally (4) there are nonarbitrary membership criterion and this criteria does not appeal to notions of "common identity."[30]

Out of all the possibilities, the last one (4) would obviously present the best-case scenerio for those who wish to remain consistent with the principles of liberalism while also advocating for immigration restrictions. Cole, however, does not believe that such a case can be made. The third (3) is the position Cole believes liberal-nationalists, such as Miller, have come to endorse. Cole rejects (3) because it is based on an arbitrary and pernicious distinction between citizens and foreigners, and in making this arbitrary distinction it sacrifices liberalism's commitment to universal equality. According to Cole, the second (2) is the best political theorists, such as Walzer, have so far been able to justify. This position, however, is based on a rejection of the *rationality principle*, which therefore makes it illiberal. This means, according to Cole, that the first option is the best and most consistent answer liberalism has for questions concerning immigration. In Cole's own words: "as it is presently constituted, liberal theory cannot provide a justification for membership control and remain a coherent political philosophy."[31]

Cole's argument is very persuasive, but some have argued that much of the argument's persuasiveness comes from its conflation of political equality with moral equality. One such critic is Michael Blake. Blake agrees with Cole that liberal discourses have traditionally conflated moral and political equality, but he points out that this conflation is the result of philosophers mostly working on the assumption that they are dealing with closed political communities. When this assumption no longer holds, as happens with the issue of immigration, the two notions of equality become decoupled. This presents liberals with an awkward situation: some persons (i.e., would-be immigrants) who ought to be regarded as moral equals are simultaneously not necessarily owed political equality. As Blake notes:

> The conventional methodology of liberalism is quite inappropriate for use when the question is not one affecting the rights of members, but the composition of membership itself. To use the political egalitarian framework to develop principles of immigration is either to assume the border as a moral watershed or to assume away potentially relevant political differences.[32]

In short, Blake agrees with the intuition behind most open-border arguments, that ". . . liberalism's guarantee of moral equality cannot stop at the border. . ." and ". . . a consistent liberal theory cannot assume away the moral status of outsiders."[33] Blake, however, disputes the extent to which Cole applies the rationality principle. Blake believes that there are things that can be morally arbitrary but nonetheless ground legitimate political differences. For example, take the case of a person from Toronto and another form Buffalo. In this case, it is morally arbitrary that one person happens to be from Toronto and the other from Buffalo, yet there is nothing unjust about using this difference to allow the person from Buffalo to vote in US elections and deny that same right to the person from Toronto.[34] Or conversely, to allow the person from Toronto to vote in Canadian elections, but not the person form Buffalo. The upshot of Blake's example is that it shows how under a liberal paradigm some arbitrarily assigned political inequalities are not necessarily violations of moral equality.

Having said that, Blake notes that: "Insisting that states do not have the same political duties to foreigners as they do to citizens is not the same as insisting that states owe nothing to foreign nationals."[35] So while Blake is critical of open-border arguments as presented by Carens and Cole, he is also not a supporter of the communitarian or nationalist positions put forth by Walzer and Miller either.[36] As Blake understands it, the communitarian/nationalist position holds that: "If immigration would undermine cultural integrity and continuity, then such immigration may legitimately be precluded."[37] On this account, the state becomes primarily responsible for protecting the interests and projects of its citizens over and against the interests of foreigners. Therefore, "If a given state does not see large scale immigration as in its self-interest, it has the moral right to refuse such immigration."[38]

Blake believes that appeals to cultural integrity or continuity can easily lead to pernicious immigration policies. For example, racist or discriminatory immigration criteria are often justified on these sorts of grounds. This puts communitarians and nationalists in a tough spot. As Walzer and Miller have shown, communitarians and nationalists believe that it is vital for a political community to have (near) complete discretion over the admission and exclusion of foreigners. This means that even if a community's reason for rejecting certain foreigners might seem repulsive (e.g., racist) to us, it is irrelevant because foreigners have no right in justice to enter in the first place. So while racist immigration policies might be rude or insulting to some foreigners, it is not necessarily a denial of their rights.

At the same time, political communities do have a duty to treat all their citizens as political equals and discriminatory immigration policies can undermine political equality even when these restrictions are targeted only at foreigners. As Blake points out: "In all cases in which there are national or ethnic minorities . . . to restrict immigration for national or ethnic reasons is to make some citizens politically inferior to others."[39] In other words, using morally arbitrary criteria (e.g., race, ethnicity, sex or gender) to exclude or admit certain groups of foreigners can diminish the standing of those citizens who happen to share (or not share) the criteria. This presents communitarians and nationalists with the following bind, the actions taken in the name of protecting the character of the community (e.g., immigration exclusions) can also work to undermine its internal cohesion by fomenting divisions along race, ethnicity, gender, or sex.

Even if political communities were precluded from using such morally arbitrary criteria in designing their immigration policies, Blake still believes that there needs to be some account as to why there is a partiality toward citizens over and against noncitizens.[40] In this regard, Blake's conclusion is in line with Cole's: there appears to be something about issues like immigration that make them a problematic fit for the liberal framework. For Blake, this demonstrates that political philosophers need a fresh start when it comes to issues like immigration. Blake says little about what this would entail, except to say that philosophers would find much of the exclusion currently employed in the immigration policies of Western liberal democracies illegitimate, since it helps to perpetuate global poverty and inequality, but also that philosophers would not necessarily find all forms of exclusion unjust.[41]

So while Blake's account here does not provide much of a normative conclusion, it does help highlight how the *liberty dilemma* returns when an issue like immigration is under consideration. On one side of the debate, there is the communitarian-nationalist view that political communities ought to have the presumptive right to control their borders and access to citizenship. On this view, if a political community lacks the ability to do so it will not be self-determined and thereby runs the risk of disintegration. If a political community disintegrates, the consequences are disastrous, not the least of which would be an inability to promote distributive justice (i.e., universal equality) and sustain the conditions necessary for individuals to be self-realized (i.e., individual freedom). On the other side of the debate is the liberal cosmopolitan view that holds that anything short of (fairly) open-borders is a violation of an individual's right to freedom of movement (i.e., individual freedom) and/or fails to give all persons equal moral consideration (i.e., universal equality). It therefore seems we are back to where we started. In prioritizing liberty over security, philosophers debating the ethics of immigration have fallen back into a *liberty dilemma*: the problem of trying to remain committed to democratic self-determination, individual freedom, and universal equality. The next section will therefore look at some nationalist and cosmopolitan attempts to resolve this problem.

THE LIBERAL-NATIONALIST AND COSMOPOLITAN RESPONSES

One attempt to give the immigration debate a fresh start can be found in David Miller's "Immigrants, Nations, and Citizenship." In that essay, Miller addresses what he takes to be the central question of the immigration debate: "How far is it reasonable to expect immigrants to adapt to existing conditions in the host society, and how far must citizens in the host society bend to accommodate 'the strangers in our midst?'"[42] In other words, what are the limits to an individual's freedom with respect to a foreign community and conversely what duties does a community have to a foreigner? While this tension has the appearance of the classical tension between community and the individual—do the liberties of the individual take precedence over the good of the community or vice versa—the question Miller is presenting is slightly different. In this case, the individual is not already a member of the community and in fact may never qualify for membership. Absent the guarantee of membership, it can never be assumed that either party—the individual or the community—has any rights or duties that bind the other.[43]

By framing the question of immigration in this way, Miller is acknowledging the worries expressed by Carens, Cole, and Blake over liberalism's inability to deal with the issue of immigration. Miller therefore suggests that one way liberalism can address the question of immigration is "by thinking of the relationship between the immigrant group and the citizens of the receiving state as quasi-contractual."[44] In other words, instead of abandoning liberalism, Miller proposes that philosophers debating the issue of immigration return to liberalism's social contractarian roots. This time, however, the social contract is not between subjects and a sovereign, but between nonmembers and members of the political community. In this way "each side claims certain rights against the other, and acknowledges certain obligations in turn."[45] This move by Miller converts the issue of immigration, which at first appeared to be a poor fit for liberalism, into something that is more palatable to the tradition. Following Rawls, Miller believes that this will convert the issue of immigration into an issue of fairness, such that "it searches for norms of fairness to set the terms on which immigrant groups and host societies interact without regard to the particular circumstances of any individual immigrant or category of immigrants."[46]

While a commitment to fairness is an excellent starting point, Miller's solution assumes, as all contract theories do, that the parties involved are somehow equally positioned before entering contract negotiations.[47] While this assumption might hold in an ideal context—where global inequalities would be minor and migration is never compulsory—it does not seem to hold in less-than-ideal contexts and most liberal accounts of immigration believe it is best understood as a less-than-ideal issue.[48] This means that the kind of starting point that Miller imagines for dealing with the issue of immigration would be a nonstarter in most cases because those entering contract negotiations would be bargaining from less-than-ideal circumstances.

In "Cosmopolitanism and Sovereignty," Thomas Pogge puts forth a framework for dealing with less-than-ideal global issues like immigration. According to Pogge, countries in the Global North (which are predominantly immigrant-receiving countries) bear certain responsibilities for the poor condition of countries in the Global South (which are predominantly immigrant-sending countries). In these cases, the duties Global North countries have incurred are negative not positive.[49] As Kim Diaz makes clear, Pogge's position is not a request for charity from countries in the Global North, but instead is a demand that countries in the Global North no longer cause any further harm to countries in the Global South and that they redress the harm they have already caused.[50]

As a way to addressing issues like immigration in less-than-ideal circumstances, Pogge proposes the idea of vertically dispersing sovereign authority.
This means that instead of understanding sovereign authority as concentrated
and indivisibly situated at one highest level, as Hobbes had proposed, Pogge
proposes a notion of sovereignty that is dispersed throughout various levels,
both above and below the nation-state. This dispersal of sovereign power, he
argues, should be de-centralized such that: ". . . persons should be citizens
of, and govern themselves through, a number of political units of various
sizes, without any one political unit being dominant and thus occupying the
traditional role of state."[51]

Those who disagree with Pogge's notion of sovereignty object that his
call to disperse sovereign power would lead to the disintegration of political
communities and thereby their ability to engage in acts of distributive justice.
Pogge's responds to this worry by arguing that the cohesiveness of a community ". . . is actually better served by a division of the authority to admit and
exclude than by the conventional concentration of this authority at the level
of the state."[52] In other words, if we concede that communities exist at levels
both above (e.g., Latin America) and below (e.g., Mexico City) the nation-
state (e.g., Mexico), then concentrating sovereign authority at the level of
the nation-state along with it the power to decide who to include and who to
exclude from membership, could potentially undermine the cohesiveness of
communities that exist both above and below the nation-state.[53]

Following this line of reasoning, Veit Bader expands on Pogge's account
by taking direct aim at Walzer and Miller's claim that states have an ethico-
political (e.g., cultural) right to close their borders and deny foreigners access
to citizenship on the grounds that doing so would undermine their cultural
homogeneity and/or democracy (i.e., self-determination). Bader's rejects this
claim because he does not think that states are in fact culturally homogeneous
or completely democratic political communities, so therefore ". . . the moral
and ethical legitimacy of their exclusionary 'right to communal self-determination' [is] severely undermined."[54]

Bader puts forth three arguments in support of this objection. First, he
argues that the phrasing itself, "culturally homogenous and democratic,"
is ". . . much too vague to be useful in either empirical or normative arguments."[55] This is because it is not clear which cultural distinctions should be
defended, when obviously some should not be (e.g., those that are classist,
racist, sexist . . . etc), and it is also not clear what type or types of democratic
closure we are dealing with. Are we dealing with a closure in which all parties
have consented, or where there is rough equality among all parties involved,
or closure when there is neither? Second, Bader claims that states have
historically done more to eradicate cultural distinctiveness, both internally

and externally, than they have to actually protect and promote it.[56] Finally, Bader argues that the defense offered by communitarians and nationalists fails to hold up empirically, as ". . . one finds even in the present world context of severe economic, cultural, and political inequalities a rich variety of newly created cultures,"[57] and also normatively, as the claim fails to take into account power asymmetries.[58]

Bader concludes that Walzer and Miller want ". . . states to be what they historically never have been—linguistically and culturally homogeneous worlds of common meaning, free associations based on democratic consent."[59] Instead, Bader advocates for a notion of citizenship that is similar to the notion of sovereignty advocated by Pogge. Bader argues that the notion of citizenship should be disassociated from ethnicity and instead should be thought of as a "multilayered concept."[60]

In summary, the cosmopolitan position offers an alternative for how to deal with immigration in a world that is less-than-ideal. It provides some good reasons for why control over issues like immigration, that traditionally has been reserved for nation-states, should be rethought in a way that better reflects the world in which we actually live. The end result, according to the cosmopolitan, would be a multilayered notion of sovereignty and citizenship that would give membership in transnational and local communities equal footing with membership at the nation-state level.

Even if this view is correct, however, it still seems very far from where, morally and politically speaking, we find ourselves today. This is essentially the reply Walzer provides in his "Response to Veit Bader." In that essay, Walzer offers a twofold response to Bader that could easily apply to Pogge as well. First, Walzer takes issue with Bader's questioning of the nation-state as the primary political unit. Walzer gives two reasons as to why the nation-state should be given such primacy: security and welfare. Walzer argues that nation-states, at least some of the time, have been able to accomplish these two tasks, while the formations to which Bader and Pogge point to as possible replacements have not shown they are up to the task.[61]

Second, Walzer defends the legitimacy of the citizenship/ethnicity connection by rhetorically asking Bader what it would mean to disentangle citizenship from ethnicity. Walzer concedes this might be possible and maybe even desirable in places like the US, "But does Bader really mean to advocate a French state, say, entirely neutral with regard to the preservation and enhancement of French culture?"[62] Walzer concludes by stressing that these two responses to Bader do not necessarily ignore the existence of severe international inequalities. Walzer recognizes these inequalities and also believes that there is a duty to rectify them, but he thinks that the cosmopolitan position goes too far in its attempts.

CONCLUSION

This chapter has provided an outline of the early philosophical debate over immigration. In presenting this outline, it has tried to make the case that the issue of immigration brings moral and political philosophy back into a *liberty dilemma*: philosophers who favor democratic self-determination believe that states should have the presumptive right to exclude foreigners; while philosophers who place greater emphasis on principles of individual freedom and universal equality believe that borders should be (fairly) open.

The next chapter will attempt to resolve this tension by presenting a position put forth by Christopher Heath Wellman. Wellman believes that legitimate states (i.e., states that respect human rights) have a right to freedom of association and that this right entitles them to exclude noncitizens (including those desperately seeking refuge). I will then outline four general objections that have been raised against his account. These objections are instructive not only as they pertain to Wellman's position, but also because they make evident some of the areas where philosophers have not sufficiently thought through the issue of immigration.

NOTES

1. Michael Walzer, *Spheres of Justice: A Defense of Pluralism and Equality*, (New York: Basic Books, 1983), 31.
2. Ibid., 63.
3. Ibid., 62.
4. Walzer grants three exceptions to this general rule: (1) refugees must be admitted; (2) prior inhabitants must not be forcefully removed; and (3) there should be no form of second-class citizenship.
5. Ibid.
6. Michael Walzer quoted in Carens, "Aliens and Citizens," 342.
7. Ibid., 333.
8. For a different and more detailed version of this libertarian argument see Michael Huemer, "Is There a Right to Immigrate," *Social Theory and Practice* 36.3 (2010).
9. Carens, "Aliens and Citizens," 333.
10. Ibid., 334–335.
11. Ibid., 335.
12. Ibid., 336.
13. Ibid., 341.
14. Walzer, *Spheres of Justice*, 39.
15. Carens, "Aliens and Citizens," 342.
16. Ibid., 343.
17. Ibid., 344.

18. Ibid., 346.

19. David Miller, "Immigration: The Case for Limits." *Contemporary Debates in Applied Ethics*, ed. Andrew I. Cohen, and Christopher Heath Wellman (Malden MA: Blackwell Publishing, 2005), 193.

20. Ibid., 196.

21. Ibid.

22. Ibid., 197.

23. Ibid., 198.

24. Ibid., 201.

25. Ibid., 201–202.

26. Phillip Cole, *Philosophies of Exclusion: Liberal Political Theory and Immigration*, (Edinburgh, Great Britain: Edinburgh University Press, 2000), 3.

27. Ibid., 3–5.

28. Ibid., 5.

29. Ibid., 203.

30. Ibid., 6.

31. Ibid., 202.

32. Michael Blake, "Immigration," *A Companion to Applied Ethics*, ed. R.G. Frey and Christopher Heath Wellman (Oxford: Blackwell Publishing, 2003), 236.

33. Ibid., 227.

34. Ibid., 227–229.

35. Ibid., 230.

36. Ibid., 231.

37. Ibid.

38. Ibid., 232.

39. Ibid., 233.

40. Ibid., 234.

41. Ibid., 236.

42. David Miller, "Immigrants, Nations, and Citizenship," *The Journal of Political Philosophy* 16. 4 (2008): 371.

43. It is worth mentioning here that Hannah Arendt is making a similar point with her brilliant insight about "a right to have rights." See Hannah Arendt, *The Origins of Totalitarianism* (New York: Shocken Books, 2004), 376.

44. Miller, "Immigrants, Nations, and Citizenship," 371.

45. Ibid.

46. Ibid., 373.

47. As was shown in Chapter 1, Thomas Hobbes argued that in the state of nature everyone is equal in that everyone is entitled to everything and anyone can potentially kill (i.e., force) or outwit (i.e., fraud) anybody else. In Chapter 2 we also saw that Locke and Rousseau also believed that individuals are all equal in the state of nature, although not in the same sense that Hobbes believed, but in a more benevolent sense.

48. See John Rawls, *The Law Of Peoples*, (Cambridge, MA: Harvard University Press, 1999): 8–9.

49. Thomas W. Pogge, "Cosmopolitanism and Sovereignty," *Ethics* 103.1 (1992): 48–75.

50. Kim Diaz, "U.S. Border Wall: A Poggean Analysis of Illegal Immigration," *Philosophy in the Contemporary World* 17.1 (2010): 1–12.

51. Pogge, "Cosmopolitanism and Sovereignty." 58.

52. Ibid., 61.

53. For an excellent defense of this position at the trans-state level see Amy Reed-Sandoval, "Oaxacan Transborder Communities and the Political Philosophy of Immigration," *International Journal of Applied Philosophy* 30.1 (2016): 91–104.

54. Veit Bader, "Citizenship and Exclusion. Radical Democracy, Community, and Justice. Or, What Is Wrong with Communitarianism?," *Political Theory* 23. 2 (1995): 218.

55. Ibid., 219.

56. Ibid.

57. Ibid., 220.

58. Ibid.

59. Ibid., 221.

60. Ibid., 213.

61. Michael Walzer, "Response to Veit Bader," *Political Theory* 23.2 (1995): 247–248.

62. Ibid., 248–249.

Chapter 4

A Legitimate State's Freedom of Association and Its Critics

In Chapter 3 we saw that even if the *liberty dilemma* could be resolved domestically, issues such as immigration revive it at a global level. At the global level, the immigration debate has traditionally broken down along two philosophical lines: those who defend a political regime's presumptive right to exclude foreigners (e.g., communitarians and nationalists), and those who support open-borders (e.g., liberal cosmopolitans). The rest of the chapter went on to show that supporters of the former tended to play up the virtues of democratic self-determination, while supporters of the later tended to play up commitments to individual freedom and universal equality. In so doing they have reintroduced the *liberty dilemma* in moral and political philosophy.

One of the more innovative attempts at resolving this version of the *liberty dilemma*, at least as it pertains to the issue of immigration, comes from Christopher Heath Wellman. Wellman has argued that it is possible for a political regime to both meet its commitments to individual freedom and universal equality, while at the same time having a presumptive right to control immigration. This chapter will therefore examine Wellman's argument and some objections that have been raised against it. The breakdown of the chapter is as follows. The first section will provide a reconstruction of Wellman's argument, while the remaining sections will outline four types of objections that have been raised against it followed by his response (or possible response) to each of these objections. While this chapter concludes that Wellman's attempt to resolve the *liberty dilemma* can survive most of the challenges that have been leveled against it, it is noteworthy that Wellman is silent on the issue enforcement, which it will be argued in Chapter 5 is his argument's ultimate undoing.

FREEDOM OF ASSOCIATION AS THE FREEDOM TO EXCLUDE

By his own admission, Christopher Heath Wellman's argument in support of a political community's right to exclude immigrants is very simple. It is composed of three rather innocuous premises:

P1: legitimate states are entitled to political self-determination.
P2: an integral component of self-determination is freedom of association.
P3: freedom of association includes the right *not* to associate.[1]

From these premises, Wellman derives the following conclusion: "since freedom of association entitles one to refuse to associate with others, legitimate political states may permissibly refuse to associate with any and all potential immigrants who would like to enter their political communities."[2]

As we can see from premise one, Wellman's argument is carefully restricted to "legitimate" states. In other words, Wellman's argument is not meant to apply to any and all political regimes, but only to those that meet the standard of legitimacy. A key component of this standard is that a political regime must be committed to protecting and respecting human rights (i.e., individual freedom and universal equality). Wellman explains why he believes this is important in the following passage:

> There is a moral presumption against political states because they are by nature coercive institutions. This presumption can be defeated, however, because this coercion is necessary to perform the requisite political functions of protecting basic moral rights. In my view, then, a regime is legitimate only if it adequately protects the human rights of its constituents and respects the rights of all others.[3]

In an effort to generate intuitive support for premises two and three, Wellman makes use of various analogies, the most persuasive of which is the analogy that likens immigration to marriage.[4] According to this analogy, the autonomy of a legitimate state is a lot like the autonomy of an individual. An autonomous individual has the right to propose marriage to whomever he or she chooses (i.e., the right to associate with whomever one likes). This, however, is not the extent of the right; freedom of association also entails a right to rebuff a marriage proposal (e.g., the right to not associate with whom one does not want to associate with).

This analogy has a lot of intuitive appeal: nothing exemplifies autonomy better than having the right to marry whom we want and by the same token not forcing, or be forced by, others into marriage. If the autonomy of a legitimate state is similar enough to the autonomy of an individual, then it would stand to reason that a legitimate state ought to be entitled to at least some freedom of association.[5] Continuing with this analogy, it seems that legitimate states not only have the right to associate with whomever they choose (e.g., have the right to admit foreigners as they pleases) but by the same token also have the right *not* to associate (e.g., the right to exclude foreigners).[6]

The obvious problem that arises at this point in Wellman's argument is that, while premise one gives lip service to respecting individual freedom and universal equality, the rest of the argument appears ready to sacrifice these commitments for the sake of democratic self-determination, thereby throwing us back into a *liberty dilemma* (and possibly even a *security dilemma*). In order to complete his argument (i.e., show that his account does indeed provide a way out of the *liberty dilemma*), Wellman must demonstrate that his view does not run afoul of these commitments. In other words, Wellman must show that his position can hold up against both egalitarian and libertarian challenges. Toward this end, Wellman goes on to consider four possible objections to his view.

The first set of objections that Wellman considers are of the egalitarian variety. In considering these objections, Wellman is careful to maintain the distinction noted earlier by Michael Blake, that between moral and political equality.[7] With this distinction in mind, Wellman begins by looking at the issue of moral equality and the possibility that immigration restrictions could undermine this commitment. In particular, Wellman considers a version of Joseph Carens's objection. Carens, as noted in the previous chapter, argued that citizenship status is mainly the result of arbitrary luck and yet has a dramatic impact on one's life. Since restrictions on migration only help to perpetuate these arbitrary inequalities, a commitment to moral equality would seem to suggest that these restrictions ought to be lifted.

With regard to this objection, Wellman concedes to all the crucial points of Carens's argument. On Wellman's account all persons are due equal moral consideration and he is also aware that there are grave and unjustifiable global inequalities that are both arbitrarily assigned and dramatically affect people's life chances. He rejects, however, the contention that these facts alone are sufficient to override a legitimate state's freedom of association. This is because Wellman believes there are important differences between "luck egalitarianism" and "relational egalitarianism." According to luck egalitarianism any unequal distribution of goods must have some rational explanation and inequalities, such as the aforementioned global inequalities, would be sufficient to morally override any regime's desire to restrict migration. For Wellman, however, this is too simplistic a view of moral equality. Wellman, following Blake claims that luck egalitarianism is guilty of conflating moral equality with political equality. This conflation glosses over the possibility that inequalities that would be considered pernicious between citizens might actually be benign when they are between citizens and foreigners.[8] For example, under normal circumstances it might be unjust to let some citizens vote in national elections while arbitrarily denying the vote to others. It is not, however, seen as being unjust to let only citizens vote in national elections while denying noncitizens the right to vote in those same elections (i.e., elections where they are not members).

For this reason, Wellman argues that moral equality is best thought of in relational terms. In other words, moral equality is not simply a matter of having an equal distribution of goods, but has other components to it as well. For example, in order for an inequality to be morally condemnable, the inequality in question must be both severe enough to warrant attention and there must also be a relationship between the parties, such that one party is the cause of and/or unfairly benefits from said inequality. Wellman claims that under this view (i.e., the relational egalitarian view) a commitment to moral equality would not necessarily require that we guarantee that no one's life prospects be affected by matters of luck.[9]

To flesh out this point, Wellman compares two different cases of unequal opportunities to go to college. In the first case, a family pays for their son's college tuition but refuses to pay for their daughter's. In the second case, one family pays for their children's college tuition, while another family does not pay for theirs. According to Wellman, both cases are examples of unequal distribution of goods and therefore would be considered morally unjust from a luck egalitarian point of view. By contrast, from a relational egalitarian perspective only the former case would be considered morally unjust, but not the latter. Wellman believes that while we personally might find both cases objectionable, only the first case constitutes a violation of moral equality, while our objections to the second case would be based on "Samaritan" concerns. If inequalities of the relational variety are the only ones that count as infringements on moral equality, then even if a concern for relational equality were important enough to trump freedom of association, it is not clear that addressing inequalities of luck would be.[10]

Luck egalitarianism might not be sufficient enough to trump a legitimate state's freedom of association, but Wellman seems to acknowledge that a concern for relational equality could be. In considering this further possibility, Wellman concedes that the world is indeed becoming more interrelated and at the same time distressingly unequal. Furthermore, he is willing to concede that the wealth and prosperity of many countries can also be directly linked to the poverty and misery of other countries.[11] In this case, a commitment to moral equality would require that something be done to rectify these inequalities, as we saw with Pogge and Bader in the previous chapter.

Yet, even in these egregious cases Wellman does not believe that foreigners have any moral claims to be admitted into a legitimate state. Wellman, adopting a version of David Miller's third argument against open-borders,[12] suggests that there are ways for legitimate states to discharge their relational egalitarian obligations without having to admit any foreigners it does not wish to associate with. For example, a state could send some of its wealth to those less fortunate, pay other countries to take in needy migrants, or even intervene in certain parts of the world to make them safer or more hospitable.[13] In short, justice does not have to be done internally (e.g., accepting immigrants), but can be done externally (i.e., exported out).

Wellman's two replies, the first addressing luck egalitarianism and the second addressing relational egalitarianism, are for Wellman sufficient to show that his position is at least not incompatible with a commitment to moral equality. But respecting moral equality is only part of the commitment to universal equality. There is still the possibility that giving legitimate states the presumptive right to control immigration could undermine political equality. For example, denying admission to immigrants on grounds that they belong to the wrong race, ethnicity, religion, and/or gender could have the effect of denigrating the status of citizens who happen to share these traits. In such cases, immigration restrictions could be responsible for undermining equality among citizens (i.e., political equality).[14]

Wellman largely concedes this point and believes that there is indeed something inherently wrong with discriminatory immigration policies, as he writes:

> [J]ust as few would suggest that individuals have a right to marry only people of their own ethnicity, culture, nationality, or character, I do not believe that a group's right to limit immigration depends upon its members sharing any distinctive ethnic/cultural/national characteristics.[15]

The problem this raises is how to reject discriminatory immigration policies in a manner that is consistent with the belief that legitimate states have a presumptive right to control immigration. This is especially problematic for Wellman because, as I explain below, he ultimately rejects a position like that put forth by David Miller while at the same time he is tempted by a position like that of Michael Walzer.[16]

As we saw in Chapter 3, David Miller also defends a state's presumptive right to control immigration and believed that it was acceptable for a state to use some discerning criteria in its admissions policy. For example, a state could more readily admit immigrants who provide economic benefits or have similar values to those of its citizens. Yet, Miller rejected the possibility that a state could use race or gender as criteria for exclusion because "to be told that they belong to the wrong race, or sex . . . is insulting, given that these features do not connect to anything of real significance to the society they want to join."[17]

While Wellman is sympathetic to the antidiscriminatory commitments of Miller, he is not persuaded by his reasoning. Returning to the marriage analogy, Wellman writes: "I would expect a black person to be insulted by a racist white who would never consider marrying someone who is black, but I would not say that this black person has a right not to be insulted in this way."[18] So while insults might be inappropriate, they are not on Wellman's account sufficient to limit freedom of association. In other words, legitimate states are not bound by justice to not be insulting.

Wellman then considers the alternative to Miller's position in Walzer's earlier account. As we saw in Chapter 3, Walzer also supports a state's presumptive right to control immigration and believes that, so long as certain stipulations were met, a state could use criteria such as race to exclude immigrants. The example Walzer used was the "White Australia" policy, where his contention was that there is nothing inherently unjust about a policy that admits only whites, so long as enough land is left for nonwhites to live on.[19] Wellman is disturbed by Walzer's position, but in returning to his own marriage analogy he finds that he cannot come up with a good reason as to why racist individuals should be forced against their will to marry someone of a different race. Similarly, if freedom of association does not force racists to marry members of different races, why should a racist state not equally be entitled to exclude immigrants based of their race?[20]

Wellman ultimately rejects both Walzer and Miller's positions and instead opts for the view put forth by Blake. If we recall, Blake's rejection of discriminatory immigration policies is as follows: "In all cases in which there are national or ethnic minorities . . . to restrict immigration for national or ethnic reasons is to make some citizens politically inferior to others."[21] This is a brilliant move. Blake's rejection of discriminatory immigration policy is different from Miller's in that it rejects discriminatory criteria, not for the sake of foreigners (i.e., not because something is owed to would-be immigrants), but for the sake of doing justice to citizens who might happen to share the race, ethnicity, religion, sex, or gender that is being used as criteria for exclusion. The force of Blake's argument, therefore, comes from its appeal to the equality of citizens, which a legitimate state is bound to respect. Even Walzer, the arch-communitarian, appears to concede a similar point when he writes that: "No community can be half-metic, half-citizen and claim that its admissions policies are acts of self-determination or that its politics is democratic."[22] Therefore, a legitimate state, in order to maintain its legitimacy, must refrain from adopting discriminatory immigration policies.

Wellman gladly adopts Blake's position on discriminatory immigration criteria and concludes: "Whether or not we are sympathetic to the idea of a state designed especially to serve a specific racial, ethnic, or religious constituency, such a state is not exempt from the requirement to treat all its subjects as equal citizens."[23] In this way, Wellman believes he has been able to successfully preserve a legitimate state's presumptive right to control immigration without undermining the political equality of citizens. This also brings to a close his larger response to the egalitarian challenge. Up to this point, Wellman has considered two egalitarian objections to his view, one having to do with moral equality and the other political equality, and has shown that in neither case is a legitimate state's presumptive right to control immigration undermined.

From here, Wellman goes on to consider the libertarian challenge to his position. Wellman again divides this challenge in two parts, both of which are epitomized in Carens's earlier "farmer example." If we recall from Chapter 3, Carens used the example of a famer wanting to hire a foreign worker and the foreign worker wanting to work for that farmer. This example was used to show that in denying admission to the foreign worker, a state would be violating the individual freedom of both the farmer and the foreign worker. In one instance, a citizen (e.g., the farmer) would be denied the right to invite someone onto his or her property (e.g., hire the foreign worker). In another, an individual (e.g., the foreign worker) would be denied the right to sell his or her labor to an interested party.[24] Carens originally presents this example as a single objection, but Wellman is correct to point out that there are really two:

> The former emphasizes the rights of those within the state and contends that limiting immigration violates individual property owner's rights to invite foreigners to visit their private property. The latter stresses the rights of foreigners, claiming that closing territorial borders wrongly restricts an individual's right to freedom of movement.[25]

After parsing this challenge into its two parts, Wellman first considers the "property rights" argument. In true libertarian fashion, this argument holds that when there is a conflict of rights priority must be given to the individual over the state. In the case of a state denying the farmer the right to employ a foreign worker, two rights come into conflict: the state's freedom of association versus the individual's freedom of association. In this case, a commitment to individual freedom would seem to entail that if priority should be given either to the individual or the state, it should be given to the individual.

Wellman concedes that this example is about a conflict of rights, but he is not convinced that an individual's freedom of association always take precedence over a state's freedom of association. Giving priority to the individual in this case would, for Wellman, be equivalent to committing ourselves to anarchy. According to Wellman, "effective political society would not be possible unless some crucial decisions were made by the

group as a whole, and . . . all areas of group sovereignty imply a corresponding lack of individual dominion."[26] Furthermore, Wellman notes that
in many instances individual freedom (e.g., right to private property) is
trumped by a regime's sovereign right. For example, people who own their
land cannot, whenever they like, just declare their land independent from
the political regime. Therefore, "if an individual's claim to freedom of association does not trump her state's right in the case of secession, there seems
good reason to believe that an individual's right would be equally impotent
in the realm of immigration."[27]

Wellman goes on to give two further reasons why an individual's freedom of association should not, at least not in the case of immigration, take
precedence over the state's freedom of association: "(1) an inability to
invite foreigners onto one's land is typically not an onerous imposition and
(2) bringing outsiders into the political community has real consequences for
one's compatriots."[28] Wellman is here agreeing with Walzer's contention that
any and every foreigner who is admitted into the political community must be
given the opportunity to become a full member and because of that:

> This invitation does not merely entitle the invitee to stay on one's land; it mor-
> ally requires all of one's fellow citizens to share the benefits of equal political
> standing with this new member of the political community. And because the
> costs of extending the benefits of political membership can be substantial, it
> makes sense that each individual should not have the right unilaterally to invite
> in as many foreigners as she would like.[29]

Wellman therefore concludes that property owner's may have the right to
invite foreigners onto their land for something like a short visit, but not to
stay permanently.[30]

Wellman next considers the "freedom of movement" argument, in particular Philip Cole's version. As already mentioned in Chapter 3, Cole argued
that freedom of movement consists of two parts, emigration and immigration, which he thinks are symmetrically related; meaning the right to exit
only makes sense if there is a corresponding right to enter somewhere else.
According to Cole, liberal theory has mistakenly treated this relationship as
though it is asymmetrical; a right to enter is dependent on a corresponding
right to exit, but not the other way around. Cole argues that there is no good
reason for holding this asymmetrical view of migration, while there is at
least one good reason for denying states the right to control immigration:
"[I]f it can be shown that the state *does* have the right to control immigration,
it must follow that it also has the right to control emigration: the two stand
and fall together."[31] In other words, consistency demands that if a regime has
the right to control one aspect of movement, it should in turn have the right

to control the other as well. Since most of us would be aghast at the possibility of a regime having the right to prevent us from leaving think here of examples like the Berlin Wall why are we then okay with it having the right to prevent people from entering?

Wellman's response to this objection closely follows the line of argument already provided by Miller.[32] Wellman concedes that a commitment to individual freedom entails the right to free movement, but similar to property rights, he does not believe that this freedom is absolute. As Wellman rhetorically asks: "My right to freedom of movement does not entitle me to enter your house without your permission . . . so why think that this right gives me a valid claim to enter a foreign country without that country's permission?"[33] And again, returning to the marriage analogy, just because one cannot unilaterally marry the person they most want to wed does not in itself deny them the right to marry.[34] For Wellman, the difference between emigration and immigration comes into focus when we look at it from the perspective of freedom of association: "one may unilaterally emigrate because one is never forced to associate with others, but one may not unilaterally immigrate because neither are others required to associate with you."[35]

This brings to a close Wellman's consideration of the libertarian objection. Wellman believes that he has now demonstrated that his account is consistent with commitments to both individual freedom and universal equality. Therefore:

> Even if egalitarians are right that those of us in wealthy societies have demanding duties of global distributive justice and even if libertarians are correct that individuals have rights both to freedom of movement and to control their private property, legitimate states are entitled to reject all potential immigrants even those desperately seeking asylum from corrupt governments.[36]

If successful, Wellman's account would resolve the *liberty dilemma* that arises in addressing the issue of immigration, but his account is not without its critics. In the sections that follow, I provide four general types of criticisms that have been raised against Wellman's account. I then provide his (or a possible) response to them. These objections are as follows: (1) the "harm objection," which questions whether an appeal to freedom of association is weighty enough to justify the potential harm selective immigration policies could cause foreigners; (2) the "bad analogy objection," which questions Wellman's use of analogies and in particular his fast and loose conflation of "intimate/expressive" associations with "innocuous" associations; (3) the "equivocation objection," which argues that Wellman's argument succeeds only in showing that a state has the right to exclude foreigners from membership, but not the right to exclude them from its territory; and (4) the "deontic ordering objection," which argues that a legitimate state's freedom of association is not necessarily a moral trump, so it can be overridden by other (and at times very similar) deontic concerns.

THE HARM OBJECTION

In "Freedom of Association Is Not the Answer," Sarah Fine argues that in being denied admission, would-be-immigrants are subject to a potential harm that is serious enough to check, or at least demand further justification of, a state's presumptive right to control immigration. Fine concedes that "exporting justice" could address many of these harms, but in making his case Wellman "does not pause to consider the possibility that the act of exclusion is potentially harmful to [foreigners] insofar as it thwarts the interests that they have in long-term settlement or in acquiring membership."[37] In other words, there are potential harms that arise from immigration restrictions, which cannot be remedied by "exporting justice." There might be reasons for why a state's presumptive right to control immigration might still override these concerns, but Wellman does not supply them.

In "Immigrant Admissions and Global Relations of Harm," Shelley Wilcox expands on this type of objection by taking into consideration the nonideal insights of Thomas Pogge and Veit Bader. Wilcox points out that the demand to enter affluent societies is today greater than the number who actually gain admission. When framed in this way, the issue of immigration poses a different problem from the one that most philosophers, regardless of whether they favor a state's right to control immigration or not, have attempted to address. According to Wilcox, most philosophers have given an answer to the question: "Do [potentially receiving] societies have unacknowledged moral duties to admit immigrants?"[38] They have not, however, given an answer to the following question: "If restrictions on immigration can sometimes be justified, which prospective immigrants ought to receive priority when not all are [or can be] admitted?"[39]

Wilcox raises this follow-up question because in reality very few international borders are totally open or closed, so she believes the real question that immigration raises is *who* should get priority in admissions criteria and *why*? On Wellman's account, legitimate states are entitled to have complete discretionary control over admissions. Wilcox, however, believes that the discretion states have over immigration decisions should be circumvented by a Global Harm Principle (GHP). This principle states that: "societies should not harm foreigners; and societies that violate this duty must: (1) stop harming these foreigners immediately; and (2) compensate their victims for the harm they have already caused them."[40] The strength of this principle, according to Wilcox, is that it is not parasitic on a freedom of movement argument or the property rights argument that Wellman already addressed. Instead, it is a claim for redress—for harm that is being or has been done—that morally entitles certain foreigners to admission.

In *Immigration Justice,* Peter Higgins makes a similar argument focusing on the less-then-ideal nature of the immigration issue. The difference, however, is that Higgins does not just focus on the harm that restrictions have on would-be-immigrants, but also takes into consideration the potential harm immigration admissions can have on nonmigrating residents of sending countries. In particular, Higgins is concerned with issues such as "brain drain" or the flight of human capital from the Global South to the Global North via admissions policies that encourage or recruit professionals to migrate. As Higgins writes:

> The emigration of skilled, college educated, middle-class professionals in large numbers from relatively poor countries harms those who remain in several ways, but, in the most general sense, it does so by undermining prospects for human development . . . [and these harms] would surely be magnified in the absence of restrictions on immigration.[41]

The loss of professionals would (and does) disproportionally harm those who globally are already the most unjustly disadvantaged. So along with circumventing a state's right to exclude foreigners (i.e., the right not to associate), Higgins's argument suggests that the discretion a state has to admit immigrants (i.e., its ability to associate) should be circumvented as well.

Wellman, however, has a response for each of these three versions of the *harm objection.* With respect to the first objection expressed by Fine, Wellman states that: "rights to freedom of association and duties of distributive justice are distinct and can be kept separate in both the domestic and international realms."[42] In other words—and allowing for the possible exception of refugees, which we will return to in the second part of this objection— Wellman doubts there are or can be any such harms that either cannot be remedied through distributive justice or, if they cannot be remedied through distributive justice, are weighty enough to override a legitimate state's freedom of association.

This brings us to the second objection, where Wilcox attempts to provide more concrete (i.e., nonideal) examples of such harms. Again, Wilcox's argument is not based on appeals to freedom of movement or property rights, but an argument based on restorative justice or the idea that certain foreigners have a moral claim on states to be admitted because of past or present harms they have caused. Wellman provides three responses to the concerns raised by Wilcox.

First, Wellman suggests that even if foreigners are in fact disadvantaged or harmed by the policies of other countries, such as free-trade agreements, it is not clear that these disadvantages or harms necessarily count as rights violations that demand compensation. Analogizing this to the case of competing restaurants, Wellman writes: "If someone opens a restaurant right across the street from mine, and my business suffers as a consequence, this competing restaurateur has clearly harmed me, but presumably she has not wronged me, and I assume that she does not owe me any compensation."[43]

Second, even if compensation is owed it is not clear why the obligation is on foreign countries and not on domestic governments to provide this compensation. Using the example of Mexicans displaced as a result of trade deals such as NAFTA and BIP, Wellman writes: "if the Mexican government believes that NAFTA and BIP are in its overall best economic interest, then it is not clear why the Mexican government is not the primary (if not sole) party responsible for compensating any Mexicans harmed by these new policies."[44] In other words, even if other countries benefit more from these policies (e.g., the US), it is the Mexican government who freely entered into these arrangements that ought to be responsible for, righting the wrongs these policies might have caused.

Lastly, even if legitimate states do owe foreigners duties of restitution, it is not clear why those obligations can only be met by taking in foreigners. For example, a legitimate state could pay a different state to take in those foreigners; it could pay the foreigner directly for the harm caused; or fix the harm by withdrawing from such agreements. Wellman likens this to the current practice of trading carbon emissions.[45] While some people might find his response to these objections unpalatable, Wellman remains steadfast that: "A state can entirely fulfill its responsibility to [foreigners that have been directly harmed by a state's action or policy] without allowing them to immigrate into its political community."[46]

THE BAD ANALOGY OBJECTION

Fine also argues in "Freedom of Association Is Not the Answer" that Wellman's argument fluctuates between two different types of analogies. The first type is an "innocuous" association (e.g., golf club), while the second is an "intimate/expressive" association (e.g., marriage or religion). Fine points out that in his argument Wellman is not always very careful in keeping these two types of analogies distinct. For example, Fine claims that Wellman's argument gets most of its intuitive appeal from the second type of analogy—a legitimate state's freedom of association being a lot like an individual's right to marry—but this analogy is based on the model of an "intimate/expressive" association. According to Fine, this is problematic because saying that citizenship is analogous to an "intimate/expressive" association (e.g., becoming a member of a political community is like getting married) is essentially to endorse what John Rawls called a comprehensive doctrine.

In order for this objection to get off the ground, it is not necessary for the reader to endorse Rawls's argument against comprehensive doctrines.[47] The important thing is that Wellman does and for that reason, Fine believes he fluctuates back-and-forth between "intimate/expressive" and "innocuous" associations in making his argument. This switching back and forth allows Wellman to both avoid the charge of promoting a particular kind of comprehensive doctrine, while at the same time buttressing his argument with the strong associational ties inherent in "intimate/expressive" relationships. This allows Wellman to get the best of both worlds. Fine concludes that if Wellman wishes to remain consistent with liberalism, the best his argument can do is show that legitimate states have the same kind of associational freedom as that found in "innocuous" associations. The problem for Wellman is that "innocuous" associations, such as golf clubs, do not enjoy the same degree of discretion over membership as do "intimate/expressive" relationships. For example, it might be unjust to force someone into marriage, but it is not necessarily unjust to force golf clubs to accept certain persons as members.

Similar to the *harm objection*, the *bad analogy objection* can also be supplemented with nonideal cases. It is important to do this because, while states might ideally be thought of as "innocuous" associations, the reality is that many people see them as "intimate/expressive" associations. If this is the case, then it is possible that there might be some nonideal reasons for states to have discretionary control over immigration. Turning again to the work of Shelley Wilcox, we see that there are usually two nonideal reasons offered in defense of a legitimate state's presumptive right to control immigration. First, it is believed that immigrants often do not integrate themselves sufficiently well within receiving societies and therefore by embracing large numbers of immigrants the conditions necessary for a liberal state (e.g., individualism, secularism . . . etc.) could get undermined.[48] Second, "the presence of ethically diverse immigrants will diminish the strong sense of national solidarity that is necessary to sustain vital liberal democratic ideals."[49] In other words, support for egalitarian institutions, such as a social safety net, depend on co-nationals believing that those institutions are in place to help "our people," and would be less likely to support those institutions if they were seen as helping mostly strangers.

According to Wilcox, there have been two ways of trying to resolve the problem of integration. One is to make immigrants assimilate to the culture of the receiving society and the other is to have them adopt the civic identity of the receiving society. Wilcox refers to proponents of the first as cultural preservationists and proponents of the second as civic nationalists. Wilcox acknowledges that most liberals recognize a problem with cultural preservationism (e.g., it can easily lead to racism, ethnic discrimination, pernicious forms of nativism . . . etc.) and therefore have tended to opt instead for the civic national model. This later model "is based on a shared commitment, across cultures, to a set of historically embedded liberal democratic principles . . . [such that] adopting [it only] involves committing oneself to the political ideals and principles upon which a particular polity is founded."[50] Those who defend this position appeal to liberalism's commitment to solidarity (e.g., social trust) in making their case that "a shared national identity is necessary to sustain liberal democratic ideals and practices in the face of the multiple identities and conflicting allegiances that characterize pluralist societies."[51] So, while liberals might reject the idea of forced cultural assimilation, they might find that the promotion of shared liberal ideals is both necessary and an attractive way of dealing with the problem of integration.

There are two arguments in support of this civic nationalist model. First, a shared civic national identity is necessary in order to sustain liberal ideals such as tolerance and a respect for cultural pluralism. The second is that a shared civic national identity is necessary for the realization of social justice in liberal states. Wilcox, however, objects to both of these arguments.

First, Wilcox thinks that it would be overly optimistic to believe that something like a naturalization process is sufficient to instill a strong sense of national belonging. As Wilcox states: "Civics and history classes would teach immigrants about the basic public institutions and history of their new society . . . but it is difficult to see how these experiences would translate into strong national identification."[52] If this is correct, then the civic nationalist position is either inadequate or is really trying to make the would-be immigrant embrace something more than a mere civic identity. If the later turns out to be the case, then the civic nationalist position is no different than that of the cultural preservationist.

A second objection that Wilcox raises is about the possibility of having a civic identity that is genuinely culturally neutral. Even if such an identity were possible, Wilcox believes that it could be used in the same way as a cultural identity (i.e., to justify polices that are inconsistent with liberal values). For example, in 2010 France banned the wearing of the Hijab in public. The purported justification for banning the religious headdress in public was that France was a liberal democracy and the wearing of this religious headdress in public places (e.g., public schools) violated liberalism's fundamental tenet of separation between church and state.[53] The justification of this ban is essentially an appeal to a shared sense of civic identity and not necessarily an appeal to culture. Yet, what someone like Wilcox would point out is that this appeal to civic identity still has the same effect as an appeal to a cultural identity: it leads to the stigmatization and discrimination of ethnic minorities.

When taken together, Fine and Wilcox's objections are sufficient to at least make us pause at Wellman's quick transition between analogies. It is also obvious from these objections that Wellman's account might be deficient in at least two regards. First, it needs to do more to justify why legitimate states should have such a strong notion of freedom of association. Second, he needs to make this case without violating liberal values and in particular without inadvertently smuggling in a comprehensive (e.g., culturally biased) doctrine. Fine and Wilcox's objections show that this is difficult, but not impossible.

Wellman responds to these objections by acknowledging that there is indeed a difference between the two types of associations that Fine points out. He does not believe, however, "that rights of freedom of association are more valuable in intimate contexts [. . . and so . . .] At most, then, [Fine's] objection highlights only that it may require more to defeat the presumptive right in intimate contexts."[54] In other words, Fine's objection only shows that "intimate/expressive" associations, like marriage, have a very strong right to freedom of association, but that does not show that the freedom of association enjoyed by "innocuous" associations (e.g., golf clubs) is so weak that it makes a poor analogy.

In defense of this claim, Wellman argues that there are many examples of "innocuous" associations, like political groups, where freedom of association is not only highly regarded, but has even been protected by legal institutions such as the Supreme Court.[55] More to Fine's theoretical point, Wellman argues that intimacy is not necessary in order to justify a strong right to freedom of association. Returning to the golf club analogy, Wellman notes that simply "being a club member gives one reason [enough] to care about the rules for admitting new members, because, once admitted, new members will typically have a say in determining the future course of the club."[56]

This would be similar to the case of legitimate states—and here Wellman would be responding mostly to empirical concerns like those raised by Wilcox—where we can put to the side most of the things we associate with a comprehensive doctrine (e.g., culture, race, religion, gender, etc.) and "there are [still] a number of obvious reasons why citizens would care deeply about how many and which types of immigrants can enter their country."[57] Maybe the most important of these reasons, which does not necessarily commit Wellman to embracing a comprehensive doctrine, is the right to determine the future of the group. As Wellman writes: "No collective can be fully self-determining without enjoying freedom of association because . . . an essential part of the group self-determination is exercising control over what the 'self' is."[58]

In short, Wellman would concede that France's right to self-determination does not justify a ban on the use of the Hijab in public spaces because in that case it is infringing on the rights of its citizens. But by the same token, France's right to self-determination would justify France determining its own admission and exclusion policy with regard to foreigners and so long as it does not violate the political equality of its citizens it is not obligated to take in any noncitizens. In other words, states like France may freely exclude anyone they choose and can still consider themselves liberal, so long as the exclusions are not based on cultural, racial, religious, or gender affiliations.

THE EQUIVOCATION OBJECTION

A third objection Fine raises against Wellman is the *equivocation objection.* According to Fine: ". . . Wellman's position begs the question whether . . . [legitimate states] are within their rights not just to control the rules of membership but also to control settlement within that territory."[59] The question begging arises from Wellman's equivocation of at least two, if not three, different types of exclusion: (1) A state's right to exclude foreigners from its territory; so preventing noncitizens from crossing its borders. (2) Excluding foreigners from settling within that territory; so preventing noncitizens from acquiring residency. (3) Excluding foreigners from membership within the political community; so preventing noncitizens from acquiring citizenship. Wellman's freedom of association argument unquestionably applies to the last of these three options, but it is not clear that Wellman's argument also applies to the other two. (1) and (2) have more to do with the issue of territorial rights and it is not clear from Wellman's argument that having the right to determine political membership is the same as having the right to keep people off a territory.

To better make her point, Fine uses the example of a private club that owns its territory and resources versus a yoga club that does not. As Fine explains:

> The [private] club members might enjoy the right to exclude outsiders from membership and from using the club's property and resources, provided that they have rights of ownership over the premises. However, while a yoga group that meets in Central Park might be free to reject prospective members, it is not entitled to bar them from making use of Central Park itself because the park is not the members' property.[60]

According to Fine, this entails that ". . . a successful defense of the state's right to exclude others from its territory could not rest on the appeal to freedom of association alone: it would require a justification of the state's territorial rights. . ."[61] Fine concludes her argument by stating that:

> If states are the legitimate owners of their territory, then there would be additional grounds for concluding that they enjoy a right to exclude outsiders from

that territory. Yet, ultimately Wellman does not appear to conceive of the state's relationship to its territory as one of ownership. . .[62]

There is, however, someone who does conceive of the state's relationship to its territory as one of ownership. In "Associative Ownership View," Ryan Pevnick makes the case that members of a state are the legitimate owners of the institutions of the state. As we will see, even on this extreme ownership model, legitimate states would still not have the kind of presumptive right to exclude foreigners from its territory, in the way Wellman believes they do.

Pevnick's ownership model goes as follows. If one does not contribute to the production of society's vital institutions, then they do not have a right in justice to enjoy them. As Pevnick writes:

> The intuition underlying [the *Associative Ownership View*] is . . . that [a group] may claim ownership over its collective accomplishments because without the contributions of members (in time, effort, and money) the [collective accomplishments] could not exist. . . . In other words, member's creation of institutions gives them an ownership claim that grounds their right to make future decisions about the shape and direction of such institutions (in other words, their right to self-determination).[63]

Pevnick goes on to provide three clarifications/implications of this view. First, that the claim to ownership is limited. Second, that by "labor" he means the creative and directive qualities that bring forth and direct political institutions (e.g., paying taxes and contributing to collective political decisions). Third, in denying people membership they are not being denied personhood. The rejection of membership only reflects that they did not play a fundamental role in the creation of these institutions.[64]

The strength of this view, Pevnick believes, is that it can justify a state's right to be democratically self-determined while avoiding the difficulties often encountered in communitarian and nationalist views.[65] In his words, the *Associative Ownership View* "explains the connection between citizens and the institutions of their state in a way that does not depend on similarities in national identity."[66] Yet, this view also does not foreclose the possibility that nonmembers might have some right to enter or pass through the state's territory. For example, a legitimate state might be entitled to deny noncitizens, even those already in its territory, certain rights enjoyed only by citizens (e.g., welfare benefits and voting rights), but its ability to deny noncitizens access to its territory would be limited. Again, even if an account like Wellman's can justify a legitimate state's right to control citizenship, Pevnick's stronger argument—stronger than Fine's in that he thinks of the state's relationship to its members as one of ownership—shows that legitimate states only have a limited right to control immigration.

Wellman responds to this objection by first addressing Fine's three-part distinction. According to Wellman states are necessarily territorial, "they are delineated in terms of land because no other means of sorting political constituents would work."[67] If this is the case, then Fine's distinction might actually be better thought of as presenting three separate questions: (1) who has a property claim on the territory; (2) who has jurisdiction over the territory; and (3) who has a right to visit the territory. Wellman's unapologetic view is that:

> Without taking a stand on property or visitation rights, my position on jurisdiction is that, other things being equal, those who occupy a territory enjoy jurisdictional rights over this land as long as they are able and willing to perform the requisite political functions."[68]

So unlike Fine's example of a yoga group that merely uses a park but does not own it, a legitimate state does enjoy jurisdiction over the territory it occupies. This jurisdiction is not derived from the state owning the territory, as someone like Pevnick might claim, but is inherent in the definition of sovereignty. So returning to Fine's example, having sovereign authority over a park is qualitatively different from owning it or merely using it, and this is what grants the state the authority to determine who may or may not enter it.

This still leaves open, however, the question of why jurisdiction should trump property or visitation rights, especially since Wellman has claimed that: "States have no compelling justification for denying individual's [specifically property owners] rights to invite foreigners to visit either for personal or economic reasons."[69] Wellman's response is to concede that legitimate states do not own their territory, but as he made clear earlier in his rejection of the property rights argument, this also does not mean that individual property owners therefore have a right to grant residency to noncitizens. The reason is that in granting residency to foreigners, individual property owners would be imposing a substantial burden on the entire political community.

But is the migration of foreigners really as burdensome as Wellman makes it out to be? As we saw with Pevnick's objection, why should foreigners be enfranchised or be given the same social benefits as those enjoyed by citizens? Wellman rejects this possibility for two reasons. The first is symbolic. According to Wellman being able to vote or have a voice in the community where one resides is psychologically important, such that its denial could make one seem or feel less worthy.[70] Second, it is unlikely that the concerns of those who are not enfranchised will be represented or taken seriously with regard to issues that directly affect them. As Wellman writes: "if the system is designed so that no one need be politically accountable to these groups, it should come as no surprise when the legal system issues policies that routinely disregard even the most legitimate interests of [any] guest work-ers."[71] This does not necessarily eliminate the possibility that people can visit and even be guest workers, but under Wellman's account they must be given membership rights after residing in a country for certain amount of time and in doing so immigrants would impose a burden on the rest of the citizenry.

In short, Wellman's response to the *equivocation objection* is that a commitment to universal equality demands that the differences between residency and citizenship be as minimal as possible, and as these differ-ences are minimized so too are the differences between a state's control over citizenship and its control over its territory. Wellman believes that if this account is to be rejected, then the burden of proof falls on his detractors to show why or how separating a state's right to control citizenship from its right to control admission into the territory does not potentially raise problems for universal equality.

THE DEONTIC ORDERING OBJECTION

According to Wellman, freedom of association gives legitimate states a strong presumptive right to control immigration such that it leads to what he termed a stark conclusion:

> every legitimate state has the right to close its doors to all potential immigrants, even refugees desperately seeking asylum from incompetent or corrupt political regimes that are either unable or unwilling to protect their citizens' basic moral rights.[72]

According to people like Michael Blake, this is partly what makes Well-man's argument so provocative. It manages to bring us to a conclusion that we normally would not have initially found acceptable (i.e., the stark conclusion) from a commitment that we do find intuitively acceptable, such as freedom of association.[73] Blake, however, believes that Wellman's argument overreaches and that there are in fact many cases in which foreigners should have a right to be admitted. This does not mean, however, that Blake rejects the idea that legitimate states have freedom of association. On the contrary, Blake believes "that freedom of association is valuable, and that this freedom [can] be a part of a convincing story about immigration, [but he is not] convinced that any state necessarily has quite so strong a right to exclude as Wellman demands."[74]

Blake's argument hinges on the claim that there are at least two different deontic (as opposed to consequentialist) ways of interpreting freedom of association. The first way, which he attributes to Wellman, sees freedom of association as a kind of moral trump. In other words, ". . . the right to freely associate means that those who interfere with our free associations *wrong* us . . ."[75] in such a way that only the most exceptional cases could possibly outweigh this right. Blake, however, favors an alternative view, which he calls the "complex deontic view of rights." On this view, freedom of association is one among many rights in a complex set of political rights where none of them necessarily functions as an absolute moral trump.[76]

On Blake's account, these political rights are ". . . derived from a more basic moral norm, which is that governments should treat all those affected by their actions with equal concern and respect."[77] In other words, the real trump in this complex set of political rights is the commitment to moral equality. Therefore, freedom of association can trump other rights but only in so far as it protects and/or promotes this normative commitment and inversely other rights can trump it for similar reasons. As Blake summarizes:

> Persons have a general, trump-like right to be treated as moral equals by the political institutions ruling over them. The specific political rights that give substance and specificity to this right, however, are best understood as complex deontic rights, and circumstances are likely to emerge in which balancing these rights is both necessary and appropriate.[78]

Wellman, however, might be able to accept that freedom of association is a complex deontic right even if it means that he must bend a little on his stark conclusion. In fact, Wellman appears to do so in responding to Eric Cavallero, who like Blake, also challenged Wellman on his stark conclusion.[79] In his response to Cavallero, Wellman suggests that he never meant for freedom of association to function like a moral trump, but instead as a kind of presumptive right. In other words, a right that can be defeated, but where the burden of proof is on those who are trying to defeat that right. Therefore, Wellman believes that "at most [arguments like Blake's and Cavallero's] merely show that this right can be forfeited in (some of) the cases in which a state's actions have made foreigners vulnerable to widespread or systematic human rights abuse . . . [but it does not show] that my general argument or conclusion must be rejected."[80]

Going beyond the concern for Wellman's stark conclusion, there is also the question of when an individual's freedom of association should trump a community's freedom of association? For example, Mathew Lister has pointed out that there are no associations more intimate than the family, and regardless of how homogenous a state is, they are much less intimate than the family associations. If this is true, then family reunification might provide grounds for a right to be admitted. As Lister writes: ". . . given what we take to be important about freedom of association, in a conflict between the largely anonymous association of the state and the highly intimate association of the family, the more intimate association deserves the greater deference here."[81] This means that, with regard to immigration, ". . . freedom of association at the state level cannot justify limiting freedom of association at the family level, even though this means allowing some significant level of immigration."[82]

In "Family Migration Schemes and Liberal Neutrality: A Dilemma," Luara Ferracioli attempts to reply to Lister by arguing that certain forms of friendship or partnerships can be as intimate, if not more so, than family relationships. If this is the case, then whatever reasons there might be to give family reunification preferential treatment in immigration policies should also count in favor of reuniting friends and collaborators across borders.[83] Ferracioli frames this as a dilemma, especially for supporters of family reunification like Lister, but this can actually be read as a criticism of Wellman. What reason do we have for thinking that freedom of association at the anonymous state level should trump freedom of association at these more intimate levels?

Wellman's response to this criticism is that it is both impractical and also imposes certain costs on fellow citizens who are under no moral obligation to bear those costs. With regard to practicality, Wellman believes that international treaties would be impossible if individual freedom of association were allowed to trump collective freedom of association. For example, if Norway's collective right to join the EU could be trumped by just one Norwegian's desire to not associate with the EU, then these sorts of treaties would be impossible. Wellman believes that we should therefore reject the idea that individual freedom of association can trump collective freedom of association and that this should hold true for a legitimate state's immigration policy as well. As he writes:

> if an individual's claim to freedom of association does not trump Norway's collective right to decide whether to join the EU or to secede from Sweden, then why think that an individual's interest in freedom of association should prevail over Norway's collective claim to design an immigration policy?[84]

Beyond the impracticality of it, Wellman also believes that there are costs to allowing people to immigrant into a country and that these costs are not borne entirely by the individual who desires to associate with those immigrants. Interestingly enough, while Wellman does not fully flesh out this argument, he might again borrow an argument from Blake. Blake has put forth what he sees as a rival view to Wellman's, but from which Wellman might nonetheless benefit from.

According to Blake, anyone ". . . who crosses into a jurisdiction [of a legitimate state] places the inhabitants of that territory under an obligation to extend legal protections to that immigrant's basic rights."[85] Incurring such an obligation, Blake believes, constitutes a cost. This cost is not monetary in nature, so it cannot simply be paid off. It is instead a moral obligation of having to protect people's human rights. Since people are not morally obligated to incur such a cost and because there is no way to pay it off monetarily, an individual's freedom of association does not seem weighty enough to override a legitimate state's right to restrict immigration. Therefore, while individuals do have a right to freedom of association (e.g., to be with family, friends, and colleagues) they do not have a right to impose burdens on others, which is what would happen if states did not have a right at some level to restrict immigration.

CONCLUSION

Christopher Heath Wellman's argument is one of the best attempts at resolving the *liberty dilemma* within the immigration debate. He argues that legitimate states (i.e., political regimes that respect human rights) have a right to be democratically self-determined and that this right entails a presumptive right to control immigration. The strength of Wellman's account is that it brings together the two sides of the immigration debate, which at the end of Chapter 3 seemed irreconcilable. If we recall, Chapter 3 ended with communitarian-nationalists defending a political community's right to control immigration based on commitments to democratic self-determination, while liberal cosmopolitans gave priority to (fairly) open-borders based on commitments to individual freedom and universal equality.

Wellman's account, however, is not without its detractors. So beyond summarizing Wellman's argument, this chapter also summarized four general objections that have been leveled against Wellman's view and then Wellman's responses (or potential responses) to these objections. While I am not totally persuaded by Wellman's response to these objections, they do seem to do enough to salvage his overall view. In the chapter that follows, I will argue that the real problem with Wellman's account is that (like other philosophical accounts of immigration justice) it focuses too much on issues of admission and exclusion without taking immigration enforcement into consideration. My contention is that the real shortcomings in an account like Wellman's are exposed when we look at this neglected aspect of the immigration debate. Chapter 5 will therefore look at the implications that immigration enforcement has for an account like Wellman's and immigration justice in general. It will also put forth what I call a minimalist defense of immigrant rights.

NOTES

1. Christopher Heath Wellman and Phillip Cole, *Debating the Ethics of Immigration: Is There a Right to Exclude?* (New York: Oxford University Press, 2011): 13.
2. Ibid., 36–37.

3. Ibid., 16.

4. Wellman borrows this argument by analogy from David Miller. See Chapter 3.

5. Christopher Heath Wellman, "Immigration and Freedom of Association," *Ethics* 119 (2008): 114.

6. Ibid., 110–111.

7. See Chapter 3, 60.

8. Wellman, "Immigration and Freedom of Association," 126.

9. Ibid., 120.

10. Ibid., 122.

11. Ibid., 123.

12. See Chapter 3 Miller.

13. Wellman, "Immigration and Freedom of Association," 127, 129.

14. For some poignant philosophical treatments on how the political standing of certain citizens can be diminished by immigration controls, see Carlos Alberto Sánchez, "On Documents and Subjectivity," *Radical Philosophy Review* 14.2 (2011): 197–205; and "Philosophy and the Post-Immigrant Fear," *Philosophy in the Contemporary World* 18.1 (2011): 31–42.

15. Ibid., 118.

16. Ibid., 138.

17. Miller, "Immigration," 204.

18. Wellman, "Immigration and Freedom of Association," 138.

19. Walzer, *Spheres of Justice*, 47.

20. Wellman, "Immigration and Freedom of Association," 138.

21. Blake, "Immigration," 233.

22. Walzer, *Spheres of Justice*, 62.

23. Wellman, "Immigration and Freedom of Association," 141.

24. See Chapter 3 Carens.

25. Wellman, "Immigration and Freedom of Association," 130.

26. Ibid., 131.

27. Ibid., 133.

28. Ibid., 133.

29. Ibid., 133–134.

30. Ibid., 134.

31. Phillip Cole, *Philosophies of Exclusion: Liberal Political Theory and Immigration*, (Edinburgh, Great Britain: Edinburgh University Press, 2000) 46.

32. See Chapter 3, xx.

33. Wellman, "Immigration and Freedom of Association," 135.

34. Ibid.

35. Ibid., 136.

36. Ibid., 141.

37. Sarah Fine, "Freedom of Association Is Not the Answer," *Ethics* 120 (2010): 338–356, 348.

38. Shelley Wilcox, "Immigrant Admissions and Global Relations of Harm," *Journal of Social Philosophy* 38. (2007): 274–291, 275.

39. Ibid.

40. Ibid., 277.

41. Peter Higgins, *Immigration Justice*, (Edinburgh: Edinburgh University Press, 2013), 67.

42. Wellman and Cole, *Debating the Ethics of Immigration*, 66.

43. Christopher Heath Wellman, "Immigration Restrictions in the Real World," *Philosophical Studies* 169.1 (2014): 119.

44. Ibid., 120.

45. Wellman and Cole, *Debating the Ethics of Immigration*, 131.

46. Ibid., 123.

47. Rawls writes that a doctrine is comprehensive "when it includes conceptions of what is of value in human life, and ideals of personal character, as well as ideals of friendship and of familial and associational relationships, and much else that is to informs our conduct, and the limit to our life as a whole." See John Rawls, *Political Liberalism* (New York: Columbia University Press, 2005), 13. Comprehensive doctrines are not necessarily bad on Rawls's account, but they are not for him political doctrines. As he goes on to say: "we always assume that citizens have two views, a comprehensive and a political view; and that their overall view can be divided into two parts, suitably related. We hope that by doing this we can in working political practice ground the constitutional essentials and basic institutions of justice solely in those political values . . ." Ibid., 140.

48. Shelley Wilcox, "Culture, National Identity, and Admission to Citizenship," *Social Theory and Practice*, 30.4 (2004): 559–583, 559.

49. Ibid., 559.

50. Ibid., 569.

51. Ibid., 571.

52. Ibid., 573.

53. "French Senate votes to ban Islamic full veil in public," *BBC News*, September 14 2010, accessed January 20, 2012, http://www.bbc.co.uk/news/world-europe-11305033

54. Wellman and Cole, *Debating the Ethics of Immigration*, 38.

55. Ibid., 38.

56. Ibid., 39.

57. Ibid., 39.

58. Ibid., 40–41.

59. Fine, "Freedom of Association Is Not the Answer," 354.

60. Ibid.

61. Ibid., 340.

62. Ibid., 355.

63. Ryan Pevnick, *Immigration and the Constraints of Justice: Between Open Borders and Absolute Sovereignty* (Cambridge: Cambridge University Press, 2011), 33.

64. Ibid., 33–36.

65. Ibid., 19.

66. Ibid., 38

67. Wellman and Cole, *Debating the Ethics of Immigration*, 100.

68. Ibid., 102n10.

69. Ibid., 137.

70. Ibid., 136.

71. Ibid., 136–137.

72. Wellman, "Immigration and Freedom of Association," 109.

73. Michael Blake, "Immigration, Association, and Antidiscrimination," *Ethics* 122.4 (2012): 756.

74. Ibid.

75. Ibid., 750.

76. Ibid., 751.

77. Ibid.

78. Ibid.,752.

79. Eric Cavallero, "Association and Asylum," *Philosophical Studies*, 169.1 (2014):133–141.

80. Wellman, "Immigration Restrictions in the Real World," 122.

81. Matthew Lister, "Immigration, Association, and the Family," *Law and Philosophy* 29.6 (2010): 733.

82. Ibid., 735.

83. Luara Ferracioli, "Family Migration Schemes and Liberal Neutrality: A Dilemma," *Journal of Moral Philosophy* 13.5 (2016): 553–575.

84. Wellman and Cole, *Debating the Ethics of Immigration*, 83–84.

85. Michael Blake, "Immigration, Jurisdiction, and Exclusion," *Philosophy and Public Affairs* 41.2 (2013): 104.

Chapter 5

The Ethics of Immigration Enforcement

In Chapter 4, I summarized Christopher Heath Wellman's argument in support of a legitimate state's presumptive right to control immigration. I focused on this argument because it seemed to provide the best resolution to the *liberty dilemma* as it arises with respect to the issue of immigration. I then outlined four general types of criticisms that have been leveled against this view along with how Wellman has or could respond to each. In this chapter I provide my own criticism of Wellman's argument, but one that goes in a different direction than the others. This criticism challenges Wellman's conclusion, that the presumptive right is on the side of legitimate states and not migrants, by considering what moral or political limits there are on immigration enforcement. By immigration enforcement, I have in mind the entire coercive apparatus a regime has at its disposal to prevent the unauthorized entry of or to locate and remove otherwise peaceful civilian noncitizens. This includes, but is not limited to, such things as guards, physical barriers, raids, detention centers, weapons, sensors, surveillance technology, and the strategies by which these are used in concert.

As prior chapters have shown, philosophers working on the issue of immigration have primarily focused their attention on questions of admission and exclusion (i.e., *who* may be let into a political community and *who* may be kept out), so a criticism that focuses on enforcement (i.e., *how* and through *what* means a legitimate state can keep unwanted foreigners out) might seem a little out of bounds. After all, philosophers often bracket questions of enforcement, at least initially, when attempting to determine who is entitled to certain rights and who is bound by certain duties. For example, in just war theory it is not uncommon to separate discussions about whether to go to war (i.e., *jus ad bellum*) from discussions about what kind of conduct is proper while fighting a war (i.e., *jus in bello*). This chapter therefore challenges the way the immigration debate has been framed within the ethics of immigration literature by showing that enforcement does matter in determining the presumptive rights or duties of immigrants.

The first section of this chapter will make the case that there are presumptive moral limitations on what a legitimate state can do to enforce its border. It will argue that in order to properly adhere to those limitations a legitimate state's immigration policy cannot be discretionary, but must instead be circumvented by such factors as economic realities, family relationships, and socio-historical circumstances. The second section of this chapter then turns to the issue of internal enforcement and the concern for political equality. That section argues that when minority communities are forced to bear a disproportionate amount of the surveying, identifying, interrogating, and apprehending that comes along with internal immigration enforcement, members of those particular minority communities become socially and civically ostracized. In other words, they are not given equal political consideration. In order to avoid such an outcome, internal immigration enforcement must be constrained so that no citizen (or group of citizens) comes to bear a disproportionate amount of the negative externalities that come with enforcement (e.g., an "equality of burdens" standard) and certain protections must be put in place that shield all citizens from the excesses of immigration enforcement (e.g., "universal protections" standard). Together these two standards create a canopy that provides all persons, including undocumented immigrants, with certain presumptive protections against a legitimate state's internal enforcement apparatus.

If the arguments in either section are convincing, then they will show that when enforcement is taken into consideration a commitment to universal equality (e.g., moral or political equality) cannot be reconciled with a legitimate state having a presumptive right to control immigration. Instead, a commitment to universal equality entails that a legitimate state's right to control immigration should be limited by presumptive duties (e.g., *equality of burdens* and *universal protections* standards) and its admissions and exclusions criteria must be determined, at least in part, by *external* factors such as social, historical, and economic circumstances. In short, when an ethics of immigration is considered in its entirety—admission, exclusion, and enforcement— the only way to consistently reconcile democratic self-determination with a commitment to human rights (e.g., individual freedom and universal equality) is for the burden of proof (i.e., the presumptive duty) to be on legitimate states and not immigrants.

JUSTIFIED LIMITS ON BORDER ENFORCEMENT

In 1994 the US began to employ a military-style border enforcement strategy along its southern border dubbed "prevention through deterrence."[1]

This strategy was put in place in response to the increased number of undocumented immigrants living in the US and in particular to the unauthorized crossing of migrants at easily accessible points of entry (e.g., urban areas along the US/Mexico border). The idea behind *prevention through deterrence* was simple. Given that the personnel and resources at the disposal of the US Border Patrol is finite and that not all areas along the border are as easily accessible, the inhospitable parts along the border (e.g., deserts, mountains, and rivers) would be used as natural barriers to prevent unauthorized entry. This strategy therefore concentrated personnel and resources at easily accessible points of entry, while at the same time paying less attention to the more inhospitable (and less easy to patrol) areas. The assumption was that the risk posed by the inhospitable terrain would deter unlawfully entry in those areas of the border. At the same time, a strong show of force at more easily accessible points of entry would deter unauthorized crossing at those points as well.

The architects of this strategy were well aware that the number of migrant deaths along the border would likely increase during the first few years of this strategy's implementation. Unauthorized crossings would obviously get funneled away from the safer, but now more heavily patrolled, urban areas toward the more dangerous, but less patrolled, mountainous and desert regions. They believed, however, that the number of undocumented immigrants, as well as the death toll along these regions of the border, would begin to decrease as word got out about the dangers of trying to unlawfully enter the US through these areas. Hence the name: *prevention through deterrence*.

Unfortunately, their prediction was wrong on both accounts. Unauthorized crossings through these inhospitable terrains, along with the exposure deaths that come with it, have remained unabated. To put this in perspective, migration expert, Wayne Cornelius, made the following observations ten years after the implementation of *prevention through deterrence*:

> the fortified US border with Mexico has been more than 10 times deadlier to migrants from Mexico during [1995–2004] than the Berlin Wall was to East Germans throughout its 28-year existence. More migrants (at least 3,218) have died trying to cross the US/Mexico border since 1995 than people—2,752— were killed in the World Trade Center attacks on 11 September 2001.[2]

According to an even more recent report, close to 6,000 migrants have died trying to cross into the US between the years 2000 and 2014 with most of these deaths being directly attributed to the *prevention through deterrence* strategy.[3]

To add insult to injury, this strategy has also been both very expensive and ineffective at reducing the number of undocumented immigrants. In 1993— the year before *prevention through deterrence* strategy went into effect—the budget for US border enforcement was close to 1.5 billion dollars,[4] while the requested budget for border enforcement for 2016 was close to 19 billion dollars. This is almost a 1300% increase![5] Yet before 1994 the estimated number of undocumented immigrants living in the US was believed to be about 3.5 million. In 2007—so thirteen years into the strategy—the number of undocumented immigrants living in the US was estimated to be about 12 million.[6] The *prevention through deterrence* strategy has therefore proven itself to be an absolute humanitarian, economic, and practical failure.

Part of the reason for this strategy's failure was its misguided understanding of migration to the US. Before 1994, most undocumented immigrants who came to the US followed a pattern of circular migration. They would work in the US for a few days, weeks, months, or even years and then return home. Few migrant workers came to the US with the intention of remaining permanently. The *prevention through deterrence* strategy disrupted this pattern of migration. As it became more dangerous and more expensive to enter the US without proper documentation, more undocumented immigrants simply began staying in the US instead of returning home. As migrants began to stay permanently they did what most people do, they set down roots in the US, made a life for themselves, and began to bring their family. So this is why instead of keeping undocumented immigrants out, the *prevention through deterrence* strategy actually had the unintended consequence of sealing many undocumented immigrants in. On top of that, it appears that the US economy needed these undocumented immigrants. This changed, however, after the 2008 financial crisis. During this crisis demand for migrant labor dropped and with it came a corresponding drop of about one million undocumented migrants. This signaled the first drop in the number of undocumented immigrants in the US in almost twenty years.[7]

The ineffectiveness and morally questionable consequences of *prevention through deterrence* are damning and they raise an issue to which few philosophers have given much consideration: what, if any, are the limits to the coercion a legitimate state may use to enforce its immigration policies and could these limits be weighty enough to circumvent the discretion legitimate states have in determining admissions and exclusions criteria? One philosopher who has attempted to address this question is Arash Abizadeh. In "Democratic Theory and Border Coercion: No Right to Unilaterally Control Your Own Borders," Abizadeh argues that:

> Anyone who accepts a genuinely democratic theory of political legitimation domestically is thereby committed to rejecting the unilateral domestic right to control and close the state's boundaries, whether boundaries in the civic sense (which regulate membership) or in the territorial sense (which regulate movement).[8]

In other words, the use of coercive force by a political regime is legitimate only when those subject to the coercion have (or have had) a voice in the direction or the shape the regime has taken. Given that foreigners have had no voice in the direction or shape that border enforcement has taken in the political communities they wish to enter, the coercion immigrants encounter at borders appears to be illegitimate.

One possible communitarian/nationalist response is to suggest that democracy requires political boundaries at some level. For example, members of one political community (e.g., US citizens) should not be free to vote in elections of a totally different political community (e.g., elections in Canada). This example seems to show that at some level political boundaries are necessary and not unjustified. These boundaries would also be completely useless if they could not be enforced (e.g., if US citizens were simply free to ignore them). Abizadeh understands this concern, but notes:

> The mere existence of a border delineating distinct political jurisdictions does not necessarily entail anything about its regime of border control, which comprises the reigning *entry policy* (how open, porous, or closed the border is) and *who controls* the entry policy.[9]

Abizadeh is here arguing that even if boundaries between political communities are necessary and justified, it would not entail that one political community has the right to unilaterally control the border it shares with another political community. Unilateral control of the border would require a further argument, which has yet to, and that Abizadeh doubts can, be offered. Abizadeh's point here is simple and yet brilliant: the principle of democratic self-determination, which has been offered in defense of a political community's right to control immigration, does not necessarily entail a unilaterally right because the control of borders affects people on both sides of the divide. It therefore requires both parties have a voice in such matters. As Abizadeh points out:

> To be democratically legitimate, any regime of border control must either be jointly controlled by citizens and foreigners, or, if it is to be under unilateral citizen control, its control must be delegated, through cosmopolitan democratic institutions giving articulation to a "global demos," to differentiated polities on the basis of arguments addressed to all.[10]

David Miller has provided a response to Abizadeh, claiming that immigration controls are not coercive (i.e., they do not violate the self-determination of others nor do they fail to respect the equal moral worth of persons). Therefore, border controls do not need democratic justification from both parties. This is because, while border regimes do prevent certain individuals from performing certain actions, they do not necessarily circumscribe the range of all adequate alternatives.[11] According to Miller, it is the later part—the circumscription of adequate alternatives—that makes coercion morally wrong and therefore in need of democratic justification. Miller continues: "By conflating being subject to coercion, in the proper sense, with hypothetical coercion, Abizadeh severs the link he is trying to forge between coercion and autonomy."[12] In reply, Abizadeh has pointed out that Miller's distinction between proper and hypothetical coercion is mistaken and if it were correct it would allow for a vast array of laws to be exempt from democratic justification, thereby undermining self-determination at a far grander scale.[13]

While this is a fascinating discussion over the nature of coercion, its focus on autonomy and democracy does not cover everything that is morally problematic with border enforcement strategies like *prevention through deterrence*. The moral wrong of such strategies has less to do with the fact that the victims had no voice in their design or implementation and more to do with the fact that these sorts of strategies fail to give them adequate moral consideration. So even if Miller is correct about the nature of coercion and self-determination (and I am not convinced that he is) the larger point that is driving Abizadeh's argument remains relevent: the lives and interests of foreigners need to be taken into consideration when determining the moral appropriateness of border enforcement—even if that means limiting the discretion legitimate states have in controlling immigration. This expansion of Abizadeh's argument therefore offers a powerful and yet overlooked objection to Wellman's argument. Using Wellman's own definition of a legitimate state, it would seem that border enforcement strategies that fail to give foreigners adequate moral consideration (e.g., *prevention through deterrence*) should be off the table. However, this can only be accomplished, as the rest of this section will show, if the control legitimate states have over immigration policy is circumvented not discretionary.

As we saw in the previous chapter, Wellman acknowledged that legitimate states have an obligation to respect individual liberty and universal equality. In doing so, legitimate states amassed some fairly onerous moral obligations. For this reason, Wellman proposed various, and at times very ingenious, ways for legitimate states to discharge those obligations without, at the same time, accruing any limits on their right to exclude unwanted immigrants. It therefore seems safe to assume that in assessing the morality of border enforcement, Wellman would continue to accept that legitimate states must respect commitments to individual liberty and universal equality.

If we begin from the assumption that there is nothing inherently unjust about the boundaries that exist between political communities (which is an assumption that can and should be challenged, especially in nonideal circumstances), then border enforcement does not on its face appear to be a violation of individual liberty or universal equality. Border enforcement becomes unjust only when it uses certain intrusive methods or practices that infringe on the liberties of individuals in morally objectionable ways.[14] For example, imagine a case where everyone attempting to enter a country, including citizens, were subjected to extensive interrogation without counsel or indefinite detention until their legal status could be positively confirmed. One does not necessarily need to have strong libertarian tendencies to see that such practices, even if everyone were equally subjected to them, run counter to a commitment to individual liberty. Under normal circumstances, justice requires that legitimate states not deploy such harsh and invasive measures—even when they are the only way to prevent undocumented immigration.

A concern for individual liberty therefore places certain moral limits on the kinds of enforcement a legitimate state may properly implement at its border. This means that the need for border enforcement is not a moral blank check for legitimate states to do anything they want. These limits, however, are still not yet limits on the discretion legitimate states are thought to have in granting or denying immigrants admission. Even if legitimate states are limited in what they can do to enforce their immigration policy at the border, it does not mean they must therefore admit immigrants they would rather not associate with.

A concern for universal equality, however, might prove to be a different story. Recall the earlier example of *prevention through deterrence*. In that case, the US government deployed a border enforcement strategy that has been responsible for an increase in migrant deaths. The dire consequence of this strategy was both foreseeable and confirmed by over twenty years of experience. In this case the border enforcement strategy was also ineffective, but what if that had not been the case? Could legitimate states be free to implement a border enforcement strategy that fails to give foreigners adequate moral consideration, if it is the only effective way to enforce their democratically supported immigration policy? If not, as I think an account like Wellman's must concede, then what could a legitimate state do to enforce its immigration policy in a morally acceptable way?

In such a case, a legitimate state seems to have four options at its disposal. First, (1) it could try to entice precluded immigrants either to remain in their home countries or to migrate to a different country. This option might alleviate enough pressure on border enforcement and thereby make it possible for a legitimate state to enforce its preferred immigration policy without having to resort to any use morally problematic means (e.g., *prevention through deterrence*). Second (2), and likely in conjunction with the first, it could modify the internal "pull" factors that are attracting precluded immigrants to its territory and in that way alleviate some of the pressure on border enforcement. Third, (3) it can limit its border enforcement to morally acceptable levels while at the same time tacitly accepting that some precluded immigrants will gain unauthorized (i.e., not official) entry into its territory. Finally, (4) it can limit its border enforcement to morally acceptable levels and at the same time change its immigration policy to better reflect internal "pull" factors that are attracting precluded immigrants to its territory, thereby alleviating the pressure on border enforcement that make morally problematic means of enforcement necessary.

In the previous chapter Wellman faced a similar difficulty as the one we are facing here, but he was able to overcome it by suggesting that legitimate states could discharge their egalitarian duties by "exporting justice" (e.g., supplying humanitarian aid, providing restitution, intervening in unjust societies, or paying other countries to take in needy immigrants). In the case of morally problematic border enforcement—when the implementation of a political community's preferred immigration policy would require not giving foreigners full moral consideration—could a similar tactic of "exporting justice" be possible? If it is, then the closest thing to such an approach would be something along the lines of options (1) and (2).

On its face, there seems nothing wrong with legitimate states trying to entice precluded immigrants to either remain where they are or to migrate to a different country. This could be accomplished in a variety of creative and non-coercive ways. A legitimate state could provide various forms of assistance or reparations to make where precluded immigrants currently reside a much more attractive option for them to remain. A legitimate state could also work with other countries, either by offering them money or other incentives, to be both receptive to and also more attractive destinations for precluded immigrants.

The problem, however, is that this tactic will only alleviate pressure from precluded immigrants whose primary impetus for migrating are "push" factors. In other words, this will only address the issue of precluded immigrants who are simply trying to escape the situation they are currently in and do not care so much where they eventually end up, so long as it is better than where they are now. Enticements to remain in place or to migrate to a different country are much less effective when the primary motivation for migration are "pull" factors. Pull factors can include, but are not limited to, economic conditions where wages are higher and the current domestic labor pool is not or cannot adequately satisfy demand, where close family relations exist (e.g., young children trying to reunite with parents and vice versa), or where migration patterns have a long and established history (e.g., circular migration, colonialism, and military interventions). In these sorts of cases, enticements are not usually enough to override the strong impetus precluded immigrants have to enter a particular country.

A legitimate state could therefore supplement option (1) with something like option (2), which is to modify the internal factors that are attracting precluded immigrants to their particular territory. This option, however, raises a whole host of other serious problems. If these internal factors are primarily things such as the economy, family relationships, and history, it is unclear what a liberal (as opposed to say a totalitarian) state could do to significantly modify these factors. The economies of liberal states are increasingly becoming more globalized and more market-based than command-based. This means that while government intervention is not necessarily inconsistent with a globalized free(ish) market economy, liberal governments do not enjoy the same kind of control over their economy as totalitarian regimes do with a command-based economic system. In short, there is not much a liberal government can do to alter the economic factors that create the demand for immigrant labor (e.g., domestic labor's inability, unattractiveness, or unwillingness to satisfy domestic demand) since these factors are largely outside of government control.

The same can also be said for family and socio-historical relationships. Once these relationships are established it is not easy (and at times might even be immoral) for a liberal government to try to sever them. For example, it would be naïve to expect that a parent would allow a lack of immigration status to prevent him or her from being with their child. In such cases, deporting citizen child (or any other close family member) might be the only way to effectively end the attraction a precluded immigrant has with a particular territory, but deporting citizens is inconsistent with a commitment to political equality, so again this is not an option open for liberal states. There are also cases where circular migration, colonialism, and military involvement have had the effect of creating close relationships between certain countries and foreigners. In these sorts of cases a legitimate state can do some things to try and sever the relationship, but the inertia of these types of relationships is not easily or instantaneously brought to a halt. For these reasons, options (1) and (2) do not provide a sufficient enough a response for how legitimate states can both maintain both their legitimacy (e.g., not employ morally problematic border enforcement), while implementing an immigration policy that runs counter to global realities.

Option (3) seems to split the difference: limit border enforcement to morally acceptable levels, while at the same time accepting that there will be some degree of unauthorized entry by precluded immigrants. This option, however, starts to take us away from an account like Wellman's. While this option does not deny that a legitimate state may attempt to deter unlawful border crossings, it does limit what a legitimate state can do in its attempts to not associate itself with precluded immigrants. So while is true that these limits do not necessarily generate a positive right to be admitted, they do seem to generate a presumptive right in the negative sense: it accepts that there are some things that a legitimate state may not do in preventing unauthorized entry into its territory. Furthermore, these limits are in place not to ensure the civic standing of citizens, but for the sake of noncitizens.

This option therefore offers a slight departure from Wellman's earlier position, where fulfilling moral obligations to foreigners did not entail limits on a legitimate state's right to control immigration. This option, however, can still be made compatible with an account like Wellman's. After all, it does allow legitimate states to maintain their discretion over official admissions policy and immigrants who enter through unauthorized means have not officially been "admitted" by the state. In other words, even though unauthorized entry of precluded immigrants is tacitly accepted on this option, those precluded immigrants have technically not been allowed in.

The problem with this option, besides the apparent hypocrisy, is that it enables conditions of exploitation, oppression, and discrimination. Undocumented immigrants, because of their susceptibility to automatic deportation, are some of the most vulnerable people in society. Their precarious situation leaves them virtually unprotected against various forms of exploitation, oppression, and discrimination by both public (e.g., tax collectors and police) and private (e.g., private employers and landlords) entities. This kind of treatment is a violation of moral equality because, even if undocumented immigrants do not have the political right to be present, they are nonetheless still entitled to have their basic human rights respected.

Some might argue that the situation undocumented immigrants find themselves in is of their own making, so a political community is not morally required to ameliorate it. A view like this is mistaken for two reasons. First, it is not clear that even those who knowingly put themselves in bad situations deserve to lose or have their basic human rights ignored. Second, even if there are such cases, the case in question is not of this kind. In the case we are considering, the political community has tacitly accepted some degree of unauthorized entry and to that extent is at least partially responsible for the presence of undocumented immigrants and whatever injustices befall them due to their unlawful status. A legitimate state could remedy this situation simply by lifting the threat of deportation, and thereby bringing undocumented immigrants out of the proverbial shadows, but this would then undermine the very discretion option (3) was supposed to be ensuring. This is because if the threat of deportation were lifted, legitimate states would find themselves associating with foreigners they would rather not associate with. Therefore, option (3) does not appear to be a viable option either.

The fourth and final option (4) is for legitimate states to limit their border enforcement to morally acceptable levels while at the same time changing their immigration policy to better reflect internal "pull" factors. The upside of this option is that, if successfully implemented, it should reduce the demand for unauthorized entry. Undocumented immigrants who currently migrate mainly due to "pull" factors will now have legal means by which to enter. This in turn would reduce the pressure on border enforcement such that morally acceptable levels of deterrence and screening would be sufficient to reduce unauthorized entries to a bare minimum.

This option marks a significant upgrade over option (3) in that it would prevent legitimate states from being implicated in the creation of an underclass susceptible to various forms of exploitation, oppression, and discrimination. It also presents an improvement over options (1) and (2) because it would deal not only with "push" but also with "pull" factors and do so in a way that would not ask government to intrude into the economy or the lives of its citizens in illiberal ways. At the same time, option (1), which entices immigrants either to remain where they are or to migrate to a different country, would not be inconsistent (and could be used in conjunction) with option (4). For these reasons, something like option (4) seems to be the best and most effective option for guarding against morality excessive border enforcement.

Option (4), however, seems to be at odds with a position like Wellman's and there does not seem to be a way to reconcile the two. Option (4) not only limits what a legitimate state can do with regard to border enforcement, but it also circumvents the discretion it has in determining for itself its own admissions and exclusions criteria. On this option, admissions and exclusions criteria have to take into account internal "pull" factors, such as economic realities, family relationships, and even socio-historical circumstances. These limitations are problematic for an account like Wellman's because they present presumptive duties that cannot be exported, but can only be discharged by conceding that there are at least some foreigners who must be granted admission (i.e., those who are pulled in by economic realities, family relationships, and socio-historical circumstances) even when the vast majority of citizens within that state would rather not associate with them.

If the preceding argument is correct, it provides an indirect argument against legitimate states having a presumptive right to control immigration. It shows that when border enforcement is factored into an ethics of immigration the only way to remain committed to democratic self-determination, individual liberty, and universal equality is for the burden of proof to be on the political community to justify any restrictions it wishes to place on immigration. This is because restrictions on immigration must be enforced and enforcing these restrictions always runs the risk of violating commitments to individual liberty and universal equality. For this reason, border enforcement must be limited, but limits on border enforcement are also what make undocumented immigration possible and sometimes necessary. While some forms of undocumented immigration can be alleviated by attending to the "push" factors in immigrant-sending countries (e.g., lack of opportunity, poverty, crime, and violence) and by diverting some of those immigrants to other more receptive countries, these actions will not be sufficient on their own. A lot of undocumented immigration is primarily driven by "pull" factors and there is little that liberal states can do to alter those factors. Therefore, an account like Wellman's must either abandon its claim to liberalism or make the concession that the immigration policy of legitimate states should not be discretionary but dictated by the "pull" factors that are drawing in immigrants.

JUSTIFIED LIMITS ON INTERNAL ENFORCEMENT

In 2008, Roberto Lovato wrote an article for *The Nation* magazine entitled "Juan Crow in Georgia." Lovato's article featured a sympathetic young girl living in less-than-ideal circumstances, who nonetheless had big dreams of one day going to college and becoming a clinical psychologist. The young girl in question was fifteen-year-old Marie Justeen Mancha. Mancha and her mother were living in Reidsville, Georgia, where the two of them had recently migrated, and were eking out a meager existence by working in onion fields and living out of what Lovato described as a battered old trailer.

In September of 2006, Mancha's dreams were put in jeopardy. As she was getting ready to go to school, armed Immigration and Customs Enforcement agents (ICE) raided her trailer. These agents had neither warrants, probable cause, nor permission to enter Mancha's residence, but they entered anyway and interrogated Mancha over her and her mother's immigration status. At the end of this interrogation the agents simply left. Mancha and her mother were not deported. Tragedy was averted because, as Lovato informs us, Mancha and her mother were: ". . . the wrong kind of 'Mexicans'; they were US citizens."[15]

The story of Mancha is instructive because it highlights the fact that not everyone who is ensnared in the dragnets of internal immigration enforcement are undocumented immigrants or even noncitizens. It also shows that in practice not all citizens are affected by internal immigration enforcement in the same way. Some citizens (e.g., Latino/as, Middle Eastern Americans, and Asian-Americans) are more likely than other citizens (e.g., white Americans) to have their day-to-day lives disrupted by internal immigration enforcement. In this regard, it seems that philosophers inquiring about immigration justice have another thing to consider. Moral and political philosophers also need to look into how political regimes locate, identify, treat, detain, and remove noncitizens within its territory and what (if any) limits ought to be placed on this exercise of power.

This concern is underscored by the fact that in places like the US almost 50% of the undocumented immigrant population entered the country through *legal* channels.[16] In other words, these immigrants went out-of-status (i.e., became undocumented) only after overstaying or not renewing their entry visa. This means that for nearly half the cases of undocumented immigration, stricter enforcement at the border would have made no difference. This point has also not been lost on many anti-immigration groups in the US and for that reason many have begun to support a strategy dubbed "attrition through enforcement."[17]

. According to Mark Krikorian, one of this strategy's principal architects, attrition through enforcement is ". . . designed to reduce the number of new illegal arrivals and persuade a large share of illegals already here to give up and deport themselves."[18] According to folks like Krikorian, self-deportation can be accomplished by extending immigration enforcement into areas that have very little to do with immigration itself, such as commandeering local police officials to perform immigration enforcement tasks, requiring employers to verify the immigration status of their employees, and similarly landlords with potential renters, doctors with their patients, and school officials with the parents of children seeking to enroll in their schools. The idea is that if undocumented immigrants are too afraid to look for work, housing, schooling or even to see a doctor or call the police, they will eventually grow tired of living this way and will leave the country voluntarily.

As was briefly mentioned in the section above, a strategy like this can be problematic in that it runs the risk of not respecting the human rights that are due to all persons, regardless of their immigration status. A further problem, as we saw with the case of Mancha, is that strategies like *attrition through enforce-ment* do not just affect the lives of undocumented immigrants; they also come to affect the lives of citizens and also lawfully present immigrants in very illiberal ways. And while Wellman's account never specifically engages with issues of internal immigration enforcement, we might still be able to gleam what an account like his would have to say about mean for internal enforcement by looking at how it dealt with a similar case. In particular, how it responded to the criticism that an account like be unable to reject discriminatory immigration policies (i.e., immigration policies that fail to give citizens equal political consideration).

Back in Chapter 4, we saw that Wellman addressed the potential for discrimination in immigration policy by grafting a version of Michael Blake's antidiscriminatory argument onto his. If we recall, Blake's argument explicitly prohibited legitimate states from adopting discriminatory admissions or exclusions criteria because in doing so a state would be diminishing the political standing of citizens who happened to share (or not share) the particular features that were being excluded or given preferential treatment (e.g., race, ethnicity, sex, or gender). So for the sake of political equality, Wellman accepted that certain antidiscriminatory limits must be placed on legitimate states' right to exclude. Wellman made sure to note, however, that those limitations would not in turn generate a corresponding right of entry. In other words, a legitimate state would be prohibited from excluding or giving preferential treatment to immigrants based on something like race or sex, but this did not mean that they necessarily had to admit (i.e., associate with) any foreigners. Given the apparent parallel between states using potentially discriminatory immigration criteria and using potentially discriminatory internal immigration enforcement, could a similar antidiscriminatory argument be deployed to condemn the use of strategies like *attrition through enforcement* while at the same time not curtailing the discretion legitimate states are normally thought to have in controlling immigration?

Blake's antidiscriminatory argument, I believe, can be reconfigured to address the potential for discrimination in internal immigration enforcement, but unfortunately for an account like Wellman's it will in this case lead to a different conclusion with regard to the discretion legitimate states should be allowed to enjoy. Unlike the kinds of cases considered so far, where foreigners are thought of as existing outside the state's territory and seeking to enter, the case of internal immigration enforcement deals with foreigners who are already inside the territory (whether lawfully or not) and are seeking to remain. This later case is more difficult to deal with because citizens and immigrants (both documented and undocumented) are not living in isolation from one another but often intermingle and live with and among each other. The task of internal immigration enforcement is to somehow disentangle these two groups without at the same time violating the rights of persons or undermining the standing of citizens. This presents a problem for an account like Wellman's because, as the rest of this section will show, the only way to ensure that such illiberal practices do not take place is to create a canopy of protections which will not only shield citizens but will also cover noncitizens (including undocumented immigrants) from the excesses of internal immigration enforcement. In short, one of the consequences of having internal enforcement respect the basic rights of everyone and preserve the equal standing of citizens is that legitimate states must forgo some of the discretion they normally are thought to have over immigration.

If we return to the earlier case of Mancha, we can see that one of the problems that arise with internal immigration enforcement is that the collateral effects of such enforcement are not distributed equally among the citizenry. These collateral effects typically and disproportionately fall on certain racial, cultural, and ethnic minorities, which in turn degrade their standing as full and equal citizens. It is therefore necessary that internal immigration enforcement adhere to something like an "equality of burdens" standard. This standard would require that any collateral effects that result from internal immigration enforcement be allocated as equally as possible among the citizenry. For example, if agents are allowed to conduct raids of private homes or places of work, then EVERY citizen's home or place of work should be as likely as any other citizen's to be raided. Abiding by such an onerous standard will undoubtedly make enforcement much less efficient and will also inconvenience many more citizens, but there are at least two good reasons for why a legitimate state's internal immigration enforcement should have to adhere to such a standard.

First, adhering to this standard would make citizens in a democracy much more reflective about the kind of enforcement they are willing to let their government deploy internally. This is especially important in a democracy, where decisions are made by the will of the majority. As things currently stand in places like the US, a majority of citizens are unaware of stories like Mancha's because this kind of enforcement rarely impacts their own lives. This disconnection between what the majority experience in their own daily lives and how the collateral effects of internal immigration enforcement affect the lives of minorities, hides the true cost of enforcement. It is therefore easier for the majority to vote for stricter internal enforcement measures that violate the rights and liberties of minorities, because they of them are either unaware or do not care about this cost and also they do not perceive stricter enforcement as in itself unjust.

An *equality of burdens* standard would reverse this situation. While the American public has shown itself willing to accept stricter internal enforcement when minorities foot the bill (as is evidenced by the fact that most legislation proposed in recent years that follows an *attrition through enforcement* strategy has enjoyed tremendous public support in the US), it would be interesting to see if such support remained strong when all citizens had to share in the costs. An *equality of burdens* standard would therefore distribute the costs of enforcement in a fairer manner and at the same time give the voters in a democracy a more accurate assessment of what stricter internal immigration enforcement entails.

Second, while meeting this standard might not change deeply entrenched social attitudes on race, ethnicity, or culture, it would prevent those attitudes (e.g., implicit biases or institutionalized discrimination) from unduly influencing the course of immigration enforcement. An *equality of burdens* standard would prohibit selective enforcement that disproportionately targets some citizens for morally arbitrary reasons (i.e., facts about them that should garner neither praise nor blame). In other words, even if increased scrutiny on people who are identified with a particular religion (e.g., wearing a headscarf or turban) or with a particular part of the world (e.g., looking Latin American or Asian) would yield better immigration enforcement results, these sorts of practices should be prohibited on account that they diminish the political standing of minority citizens who happen to share those features. In short, a commitment to political equality should never be traded away for any supposed benefits to enforcement.

But while something like an *equality of burdens* standard would be a necessary part of a just internal immigration enforcement scheme, it would not itself be sufficient—at least not to insure that basic liberties (i.e., individual freedom) are not violated. For example, certain intrusive inspections might be okay at points of entry, but when conducted internally or done too frequently could easily constitute a rights violation. For example, routine car inspections might be acceptable at points of entry, but random car inspections on the highway (especially if done frequently) might prove to be too excessive in a liberal democracy. Similarly, standard requests to verify one's immigration status might be okay at points of entry, but excessive when applied often on the streets of a liberal democracy and especially at one's home. The idea here is that even when citizens are asked to share equally in the burdens of enforcement, there are some costs that no legitimate state should ask their citizens to bear. In other words, government actions such as indefinite detention and unreasonable searches and seizures are not simply unjust when the burdens are not shared equally. Those sorts of actions are always and in-themselves unjust. Another way of putting the same point is that even if citizens shared equally all the burdens of internal immigration enforcement, some forms of enforcement would still be too excessive and should always remain off the table.

So along with an *equality of burdens* standard, it would be necessary for legitimate states to meet a "universal protections" standard. Meeting this standard would require that all persons be reasonably protected from excessive internal immigration enforcement. This standard would complement the *equality of burdens* standard by putting in place certain mechanisms for oversight against excessive enforcement. Specifying what particular type of oversight or which particular restrictions would be demanded by a *universal protections* standard, is difficult to pinpoint exactly given that different political communities have their own unique set of circumstances and challenges.

With that being said, there seems to be at least one general oversight that a *universal protections* standard should always adhere to: there must always be a presumption of innocence. In the immigration context this would mean that all persons present should initially be treated as though they are lawfully present until their status has been confirmed to be irregular and even then should still have their dignity and rights respected as human beings. This general oversight is based on the same idea that people should be considered innocent until proven guilty; the famous Blackstone formulation that it is better to let many guilty people to go free than for one innocent person to be found guilty. This is an important point to keep in mind when we consider that places like the US have in the past wrongfully deported of some its own citizens and people who otherwise were eligible to remain in the country. In one case, the wrongfully deported citizen was a developmentally disabled man, whose return trip was traumatic and very easily could have ended in tragedy.[19] Another case did end in tragedy, when the wrongfully deported person died in a fire inside a Honduran jail where the Honduran immigration agency was holding him.[20]

So if a legitimate state's immigration enforcement were to adhere to something like a *universal protections* standard and the presumption of innocence that such a standard always entails, it would need to give all persons present, regardless of their immigration status, such basic protections as the right to due process, equal protection under the law, freedom from unreasonable searches and seizures, a right to a court appointed attorney, and protection from indefinite detention.[21] Protections like these are essential in immigration cases because without them immigration controls could easily infringe on the basic liberties of persons and could also lead to accidently deportations. These protections are not the only ones that would satisfy the *universal protections* standard, and it is likely that more, rather than less, protections would be necessary in order to adequately meet this standard in most cases. But even just the protections mentioned here are enough to illustrate the following point: protecting basic liberties from potential governmental excesses puts the burden on legitimate states to insure that their immigration enforcement practices do not overreach, especially internally, and this can be done only by putting adequate protections in place.

When taken together, the two standards outlined above form a canopy of protections that ameliorate, if not eliminate, the threat of internal immigration enforcement infringing on the basic liberties of persons or undermining the standing of citizens. For example, the raid that took place in Mancha's home would have been prohibited under these two standards. In that case, ICE agents would have (1) needed to have a warrant in order to enter Mancha's home, as would be demanded by something like a *universal protections* standard and (2) such a warrant could not have been obtained by ICE, under an *equality of burdens* standard, if its only reason for targeting Mancha and her mother was their ethnicity or occupation.

Similarly, this canopy of protections would prohibit most other nefarious aspects of strategies like *attrition through enforcement*. For example, the commandeering of police officers to perform immigration enforcement duties, a common feature of many recent internal immigration enforcement strategies,[22] would be prohibited under this canopy of protections. There are at least two reasons as to why. First, when police are required or have the power to enforce immigration laws, certain citizens are less likely to come forward to report crimes. Currently, many households are of "mixed status," that is households where the immigration status of individual household members can vary from undocumented to full citizen. Victims of crimes who happen to be living in mixed-status households are often hesitant to call police when they believe that the police will or has the power to deport members of their household. This indirect consequence of internal enforcement is not only a violation of the *universal protections* standard, but also the *equality of burdens* standard, since it affects only certain citizens and usually for morally arbitrary reasons.

A second reason is that the safety of a community is dependent on the lawful cooperation of all persons present, regardless of their immigration status. It is not uncommon, for example, that undocumented immigrants are themselves the victims of crime or are witnesses to crimes. In either case, it is important that all persons present be assumed to be lawfully present by police in order for officers to adequately perform their primary function, which is to protect, serve, and fulfill the rights of everybody in the community. In this case the *universal protections* standard would apply and prohibit police from performing immigration enforcement duties, even when that prohibition would undermine the effectiveness of the current immigration policy.

These sorts of arguments can be extended to cases of employment, renting a home, enrolling children in school, and many other everyday activities that have recently been incorporated as part of internal immigration enforcement strategies.[23] What each of these prohibitions on internal enforcement show is that the kinds of protections needed to avoid the potentially pernicious aspects of enforcement are ones that not only cover citizens, but also extends to everyone present, including undocumented immigrants. This canopy of protections is therefore a presumptive check on a legitimate state's ability to control immigration. It makes it such that there are certain things a legitimate state, all things being equal, is prohibited from doing even when failing to do so negatively impacts its ability to control immigration. In the examples just provided, we see that a legitimate state is prima facie prohibited from using its own police force as part of its immigration enforcement scheme and also that the power immigration enforcement officers have must be curtailed in ways that inhibit their ability to control immigration (e.g., they must get warrants and have substantial probable cause). These sorts of protections do not necessarily generate positive rights to admission, but they are nonetheless overriding negative prohibitions that, all things being equal, protect undocumented immigrants from a legitimate state's enforcement mechanism.

This is therefore the difference between using Blake's antidiscriminatory argument for cases like those in Chapter 4 (e.g., those dealing with admission and exclusion criteria) and then redeploying it for cases concerning internal immigration enforcement as we have here. These latter cases do not have the same amount flexibility as the earlier cases. In Blake's original argument, antidiscriminatory commitments never compromised a legitimate state's ability to disassociate from noncitizens. A legitimate state was merely prohibited from using discriminatory criteria for admitting or excluding foreigners. With respect to internal immigration enforcement, a state is much more restricted in what it can do to disassociate itself from noncitizens—at least in ways that are consistent with prior liberal commitments. If the argument provided above is correct, a legitimate state will at times have to associate with undocumented immigrants (e.g., either through its police force or public schools), but its liberal commitments—enshrined in the *equality of burdens* and *universal protections* standards—will prohibit it from using those particular interactions as occasions to remove them. A legitimate state will be in a bizarre position of having to actively restrict itself, because of its liberal commitments, from fully enforcing its own immigration laws. And while this does not necessarily generate a positive right to immigrate, it nonetheless provides presumptive negative rights that shield immigrants from internal immigration enforcement.

OBJECTIONS TO A MINIMALIST DEFENSE OF IMMIGRANT RIGHTS

When taken together, these last two sections provide a basis for what I call a minimalist defense of immigrant rights. It is a defense of immigrant rights in that it puts the presumptive duty on political communities (in this case legitimate states) and not on immigrants. If there are to be any restrictions on immigration, it is incumbent upon political communities to justify the need for such restrictions and explain how it can enforce such restrictions without in turn generating further injustices. This account is minimalist in the sense that it aims to provide a floor, but has little to say about the ceiling. In other words, my view is consistent with (and even sympathetic to) an open-borders position, but does not necessarily require open-borders for minimum justice to be met.

The strength of this view, and the reason why moral and political philosophers ought to adopt it, is that it offers the only consistent way out of both the *security* and *liberty dilemmas*, at least with respect to the debates surrounding immigration. This view, however, is not without its critics and so this final section will be devoted to looking at two possible objections. The first objection is that the minimalist defense concedes too much to individual liberty and universal equality and so does not adequately account for a political community's security or democratic self-determination. I call this the "conservative" objection. The second objection is that this view does not go far enough in defending immigrants or diagnosing current immigration injustices. It argues that something like my minimalist view could be adopted and yet it would not do enough to end the exploitation and oppression of immigrants—especially undocumented immigrants. I call this the "radical" objection.

My response to the first objection, the *conservative* objection, really began back in Chapter 1. There I tried to show why an overemphasis on security only traps us in a *security dilemma*. As I argued toward the end of that chapter, I believe that a constitutional democracy—a form of sovereignty that gives priority to liberty—is really the best hope we have for avoiding this dilemma altogether. It provides a political regime with sufficient enough sovereignty that, like the Westphalian nation-state, it can avoid the threat of a Hobbesian *state of nature*. But unlike a Westphalian nation-state, this kind of political regime does not have authoritarian powers. In constitutional democracies, those subject to the power of the sovereign (including undocumented immigrants) are not placed completely outside the realm of legal protections. Constitutional democracies in fact are designed to avoid Agambenian *states of exception* by providing individuals with basic rights and by dispersing political power through various systems of checks-and-balances.

This, however, brings up the issue of democratic self-determination. Political regimes, such as constitutional democracies, are legitimate only in so far as they are sufficiently democratic and self-determined. The view I advocate seems to sacrifice a lot of democratic self-determination for the sake of noncitizens (i.e., nonmembers). This part of the objection is one that I tried to address in the chapters that followed Chapter 1. As we saw beginning in Chapter 2, the issue of political legitimacy is complicated. Democratic self-determination is central to any account of political legitimacy, but so are commitments to individual freedom and universal equality. Constitutional democracies attempt to hold these different commitments together so that neither gets sacrificed too much in efforts to obtain the others. What I have tried to show is that a robust notion of democratic self-determination is not only consistent with a minimalist account of immigrant rights, but actually that this minimalist account is entailed in a proper accounting of democractic self-determination. Conversely, the kind of democratic self-determination that would be required to defend a political community's presumptive right to control immigration would be inconsistent with commitments to individual freedom and universal equality (i.e., it asks us to sacrifice too much of them), and therefore would make it a poor fit for a legitimate state.

In short, the problem with the *conservative* objection is that it is self-defeating. It asks us to sacrifice our liberal commitments (which keep us safe from authoritarian regimes) for the sake of security or self-determination (presumably from other states or foreigners). Security and self-determination, however, has always been undergirded, not undermined, by commitments to individual freedom and universal equality. So the only consistent way to avoid the *security dilemma*, I believe, is through a constitutional democracy and the only way to obtain a constitutional democracy is to resolve the *liberty dilemma*. If the *liberty dilemma* is to be resolved, a regime must respect the human rights of all persons, including precluded and undocumented immigrants, and this will entail some strenuous limits on its ability to exclude or remove unwanted foreigners. This is part of the price of taking the liberty concern seriously, which again is the only way we get out of the *security dilemma*.

Assuming that a constitutional democracy is desirable, possible, and can address the *conservative* objection; there is still another objection to consider. This objection holds that a minimalist defense of immigrant rights does not go far enough. That it gives only the illusion of justice to immigrants, when in fact it could do more harm than good by giving immigrants and their communities a false sense of security. For example, Ernesto Rosen Velásquez has suggested something along these lines when he writes that:

> we should consider immigration matters in terms of states of violence as a way to move beyond notions of states that take for granted an idealized political ontology, statist narratives, and assume histories that occlude colonialism and the violence constitutive of states. Introducing a notion of states of violence into the conversation allows us to make a distinction between states of violence and a Wellman-type narrow notion of states as nonconsensual coercive institutions where violence is marginal. This distinction enables us to get a clearer grasp of the underlying divergences in the immigration debate and hopefully opens up conceptual paths to begin to think about unraveling these pressing, complex immigration problems.[24]

What Velásquez is suggesting is that when philosophers appeal to something like "constitutional democracies" or "legitimate states" they are—either purposefully or inadvertently—covering over many of the injustices that motivate the immigration debate in the first place and that should be central to any theoretical analysis of immigration. He would argue that actually existing states are not and have never been democratic or legitimate in the way philosophers use the terms. In actuality, immigrant-receiving states (i.e., actually existing liberal democracies) have historically benefited from the exploitation and oppression of what are today immigrant-sending countries (i.e., developing countries in the Global South). When we understand immigration in this context it becomes easier to see why there is such disdain for certain immigrants (e.g., Latin American, Middle Eastern, or Asian American to the US) while at the same time other immigrants get celebrated as part of the national fabric (e.g., European immigrants to the US). Taking this kind of theoretical approach also helps to better prescribe ways to redress these sorts of injustices.

According to an account like Velásquez's, these explanatory and critical tasks can only be accomplished if we begin with something like a "states of violence" model instead of the more idealized state models that we have primarily been working with in this book. This is not because people aspire to live in states of violence, in the way people might aspire to live in a democratic or legitimate state, but because we currently find ourselves living in a state of violence and not in a truly democratic or legitimate state. The democratic or legitimate state model is therefore inept at performing the kind of diagnostic and critical tasks that are needed to truly address the current immigration crisis. My minimalist defense of immigrant rights might therefore be theoretically sufficient to undermine a Wellman-type defense of immigration restrictions, but as Velásquez would argue it does nothing to help diagnose, critique, or resolve any of the immigration injustices that are occurring in the here and now (i.e., in a state of violence).

My response to this criticism is threefold. First, I would like to concede that something like the state of violence model might better describe today's globally dominant states and that this model operates under a very different kind of logic than the democratic or legitimate state models. This concession, however, is not necessarily incompatible with my view as much as it is a challenge to the current artificial parameters that have been set on the philosophical debate over immigration in general. I see my minimalist defense of immigrant rights as working in parallel and not necessarily in opposition to an account like Velásquez's. To my way of thinking, this is not a situation of having to choose between an idealized state model and an "actually existing" state model, but of understanding what task we need our models to perform. Using an idealized state model allows us to see why immigration restrictions, are fundamentally problematic and why this is so in any and all possible worlds. At the same time, something like the state of violence model helps to explain how the injustice of our particular world came to be, how it operates, and what can be done about it. If this is correct, then it's not so much an issue of the state of violence model being better or worse than the democratic or legitimate state model (as the objection might have initially seemed to imply), but about using the right model for the right job.

Second, even though my argument concludes with only a minimalist defense of immigrant rights, this minimal conclusion is not nothing. The minimalist defense offers a compelling challenge to supporters of a political community's right to control immigration; not only in ideal cases, but as many of my examples hopefully showed, in nonideal cases too. The minimal rights that come out of an approach like mine provides some strong reasons as to why all states (including the ones we currently live in) should not engage in strategies like *prevention through deterrence* or *attrition through enforcement*, which accounts like Velásquez's often point to as specific examples of nonideal injustices. In short, the goal of the minimalist approach to immigration justice is emphatically not to put a cap on immigrant rights or the responsibility real existing states might have to foreigners, but to work to create a solid theoretical foundation on which a larger defense of immigrant rights and a critique of unjust regimes can be mounted. The hope is that this foundation will continue to grow and that more expansive configurations of immigrant rights will eventually emerge from it.

Lastly, there is at least one substantial theoretical advantage my approach has over an approach like that of Velásquez. The minimalist approach does not make immigrant rights dependent or contingent upon something else while an approach like Velásquez's seems to suggest that the rights immigrants have to be admitted are based on restorative pleas for prior or ongoing injustices. Conversely, this approach also holds that a state has no right to exclude foreigners only in so far as it has or is committing injustices. In both of these cases, the rights of immigrants or the duties of states are contingent upon either prior or ongoing injustices. This tells us nothing however about where the right or duty might be in the absence of these injustices or what happens when prior injustices have been satisfactorily redressed (e.g., if Wellman's "exporting justice" comes to fruition). By contrast, my view is unconditional, immigrants have rights and states have duties regardless of how just or unjust a state may be. In other words, the injustices of states may help bolster my defense of immigrant rights, but in no way is my defense dependent upon those injustices. This, I believe, deepens the case for immigrant rights and makes it much less assailable.

CONCLUSION

The arguments presented in the first two sections of this chapter focused on Christopher Heath Wellman's freedom of association argument. Wellman's argument was singled out because it is one of the best attempts at resolving the *liberty dilemma* within the immigration debate. My objection to Wellman's argument, which is different from other criticisms that have already been leveled against it, is that when immigration enforcement is taken into consideration his argument cannot hold up. Border and internal enforcement present threats to individual freedom and universal equality that legitimate states must guard against. In order to develop a principled way of guarding against these threats, the control legitimate states are normally thought to have over designing and implementing their immigration policy will be bounded and not discretionary. This is a position that I call a minimalist defense of immigrant rights.

I recognize that this minimalist position might not give everyone everything they want—conservatives will object that too much security and self-determination is compromised, while radicals will say that it does not do or go far enough—but I maintain that it will give us what we need, which is a way to consistently avoid both the *security* and *liberty dilemmas* within the immigration debate. While I feel that my position holds the most promise, there is still the question of what such a position would mean for actual immigration reform in a world like ours. I do not have the space in this book, not do I know that it would be possible, to provide a fully robust immigration reform proposal that would work for all places and at all times, but in the conclusion to this book I would like to at least provide an outline for what a framework for just immigration reform would look like, based on an account like the one I have provided so far.

NOTES

1. "Immigration Enforcement Within the United States," Congressional Research Service, *The Library of Congress*, April 6, 2006, Accessed December 21, 2014, http://www.fas.org/sgp/crs/misc/RL33351.pdf

2. Wayne A. Cornelius, "Controling 'Unwanted' Immigration: Lessons From the United States, 1993–2004," *Journal of Ethnic and Migration Studies* 31.4 (2005): 783.

3. Tara Brian and Frank Laczko Ed., "Fatal Journeys: Tracking Lives Lost during Migration," *International Organization for Migration* 1.1 (2014): 54.

4. "Immigration and Naturalization Service," *Department of Justice* Accessed November 19, 2015. http://www.justice.gov/archive/jmd/1975_2002/2002/html/page104-108.htm

5. "Budget-in-Brief Fiscal-Year 2016," *Department of Homeland Security* pdf Accessed November 19, 2015. http://www.dhs.gov/sites/default/files/publications/FY_2016_DHS_Budget_in_Brief

6. "Unauthorized Immigrant Population Trends for States, Birth Countries and Regions," *Pew Research Center,* December 11, 2014. Accessed November 19, 2015. http://www.pewhispanic.org/2014/12/11/unauthorized-trends/#All

7. Ibid.,

8. Arash Abizadeh, "Democratic Theory and Border Coercion: No Right to Unilaterally Control Your Own Borders," *Political Theory* 36.1 (2008): 38.

9. Ibid., 43.

10. Ibid., 54.

11. David Miller, "Why Immigration Controls Are Not Coercive: A Reply to Arash Abizadeh," *Political Theory* 38.1 (2010).

12. Ibid., 116.

13. Arash Abizadeh, "Democratic Legitimacy and State Coercion: A Reply to David Miller," *Political Theory* 38.1 (2010).

14. For a different, but compatible, account of how political boundaries can become unjust see Grant J. Silva, "On the Militarization of Borders and the Juridical Right to Exclude," *Public Affairs Quarterly* 29.2 (2015).

15. Roberto Lovato, "Juan Crow in Georgia" *The Nation*, May 26, 2008. http://www. thenation.com/article/juan-crow-georgia Accessed December 21, 2014.

16. See Ted Robbins, "Nearly Half of Illegal Immigrants Overstay Visas," *NPR*, June 14, 2006, Accessed September 15, 2011, http://www.npr.org/templates/story/story.php?storyId=5485917

17. Jessica Vaughan, "Attrition Through Enforcement: A Cost-Effective Strategy to Shrink the Illegal Population," *Center for Immigration Studies*, April 2006, Accessed September 15, 2011, http://www.cis.org/Enforcement-IllegalPopulation

18. Mark Krikorian, "Attrition Through Enforcement Will Work," *San Diego Union Tribune*, April 2, 2006, Accessed May 23, 2015, http://www.utsandiego.com/uniontrib/20060402/news_mz1e02krikor.html

19. Kemp Powers, "Group says U.S. citizen wrongly deported to Mexico" *Reuters*, June 11, 2007, Accessed May 10, 2012, http://www.reuters.com/article/2007/06/11/us-usa-immigration-deportation-idUSN1118919320070611

20. Ruxandra Guidi, "Honduran LA resident accidentally deported, then dies in prison fire" *Southern California Public Radio*, March 2, 2012, Accessed May 10, 2012, http://www.scpr.org/news/2012/03/02/31481/honduran-resident-los-angeles-wrongfully-deported

21. For an excellent argument on how the detention of undocumented immigrants constitutes a rights violation see Stephanie J. Silverman, "Detaining Immigrants and Asylum Seekers: A Normative Introduction," *Critical Review of International Social and Political Philosophy* 17.5 (2014).

22. In the US, federal law currently allows for immigration enforcement and local law enforcement to form a partnership under a program called "Secure Communities." For more information on this specific program see http://www.ice.gov/secure_communities/. Also, this linking up of local law enforcement with immigration enforcement has appeared in various state immigration bills. The most notorious of these being Arizona's SB 1070. See State of Arizona Senate, Forty-Ninth Legislature, Second Regular Session 2010, Senate Bill 1070.

23. For a more detailed argument along these lines see Joseph H. Carens, "The Rights of Irregular Migrants," *Ethics & International Affairs* 22.2 (2008).

24. Ernesto Rosen Velásquez, "States of Violence and the Right to Exclude" *Journal of Poverty*, DOI: 10.1080/10875549.2016.1186777: 19.

Conclusion

Toward a Just Framework for Immigration Reform

In this book, I have tried to show how the issue of immigration should be viewed as central to Western moral and political philosophy and why it should not be treated as merely a problem of "applied ethics." I did this by showing how the *security* and *liberty dilemmas* have always been at the heart of Western moral and political philosophy and how they reemerge when the issue of immigration is taken into consideration. I defended the claim that the only way to adequately resolve both of these dilemmas would entail immigrants having presumptive rights over a political community's ability to exclude or remove them. To be clear, these presumptive rights are defeasible, meaning they can be defeated under certain circumstances, namely if the countering interests or reasons are weighty enough, but in all cases the burden of proof (i.e., the presumptive duty) is on legitimate states and not immigrants.

The argument in defense of this claim began back on Chapter 1 with an outline of the *security dilemma* as it has occurred in the immigration policies of places like the US. I argued that these policies give priority to the security concern over the liberty concern and that this has meant that political regimes are thought to have an unrestricted right to control immigration. The reasoning has been that without this unrestricted right to control immigration, a political regime risks falling into a Hobbesian "state of nature." Yet, when this Hobbesian solution to the *state of nature* is followed to its logical conclusion, we find that it tends to lead toward a totalitarian regime. A totalitarian regime may be good at keeping a political community safe from certain threats, but these sorts of regimes are always in themselves a threat to security. The threat they pose is perhaps best exemplified by Giorgio Agamben's notion of the "state of exception" or the condition of being vulnerable to an awe-inspiring political power that would never exist in a *state of nature*. In short, the immigration policies of places like the US have been stuck trying to avoid falling into a *state of nature* while at the same time generating *states of exception*.

Toward the end of Chapter 1, I presented the possibility that the best way to resolve the *security dilemma* would be to give priority to the liberty concern over the security concern. Specifically, I argued that a Philadelphia model of sovereignty (i.e., a constitutional democracy) should be preferred over a Westphalian model of sovereignty. In other words, a form of sovereignty that can ameliorate the *security dilemma* (i.e., avoid the threats of both the *state of nature* and *state of exception*) would be one that breaks up political power through a system of checks-and-balances and that respects the basic liberties of individuals.

This seemed like a very promising solution but as we later saw in Chapter 2, constitutional democracy is dependent on bringing together two very distinct notions of liberty (i.e., negative and positive) that do not always cohere well together. This tension is what brings about the *liberty dilemma*. Negative liberty is essential to any set of basic liberties since it gives priority to individual freedom, but it tends to do so only at the expense of universal equality and democratic self-determination. Positive liberty is necessary to promote democratic self-determination and universal equality, but it also seems to do this at the expense of individual freedom. Yet, in a constitutional democracy all three commitments—democratic self-determination, individual freedom and universal equality—must be brought together.

In the second half of Chapter 2, I went on to argue that John Rawls's two principles of justice, based on Kant's notion of autonomy, were enough to overcome the *liberty dilemma* and address utilitarian and Marxist objections to Kant. The problem with the Rawlsian solution, however, is that one of its most fundamental assumptions is that political communities should be thought of as already bounded—they are societies we enter only by birth and exit only in death. This assumption is not so much a problem when the issue at hand is domestic justice, but it makes Rawls's view largely ineffective when the issue is something like immigration. The *liberty dilemma* therefore returns to moral and political philosophy in a new form when the question of immigration justice is taken up.

In Chapter 3, I provided an outline of the early philosophical debate over immigration. In doing so, I showed how this was in fact a re-instantiation of the *liberty dilemma*, with philosophers favoring one side of the dilemma or the other. For example, nationalist-communitarians tended to favor democratic self-determination and political equality, while liberal cosmopolitans tended to favor individual freedom and moral equality.

In Chapter 4, I then outlined an attempt by Christopher Heath Wellman to overcome this dilemma. Wellman made the case that legitimate states (i.e., states that respect individual freedom and universal equality) have a presumptive right to control immigration and that this right is based on their collective freedom of association (i.e., democratic self-determination). In the second half of that chapter I went on to present four general criticisms that have been leveled against Wellman's account and how he has (or could have) responded to each of them.

In Chapter 5, I presented my view, which is that even if Wellman's account can address those other criticisms, it does not hold up when it has to take enforcement into account. I argued that border and internal enforcement present different sorts of challenges to individual freedom and universal equality than Wellman has so far considered and they cannot be addressed without in turn circumventing a legitimate state's right to control immigration. These challenges therefore put an account like Wellman's in a difficult position: it must either abandon its claim to liberalism (i.e., to commitments to individual freedom and universal equality) or concede that immigrants, including undocumented immigrants, have some presumptive rights that outweigh a legitimate state's right to control immigration.[1] The argument I have made throughout this book is that the best alternative would be the latter, giving immigrants presumptive rights and placing the burden of proof on political communities (especially legitimate states) with respect to the issue of immigration. This is a view I have dubbed the minimalist defense of immigrant rights.

Regardless of whether my ultimate conclusion is correct or not, the arguments provided in this book so far have at least shown that the issue of immigration is more than a problem of applied ethics, but is in fact an extension of the important debates that have dominated Western moral and political philosophy since at least the modern period. What this book so far has not done is show how the philosophy of immigration can contribute to the pressing immigration debates taking place today and in particular what policy recommendations an account like this would entail. Therefore, in the concluding section of this concluding chapter, I would like to offer a brief outline of what a just immigration reform policy would look like if it were to follow the minimalist approach I have been endorsing.

A FRAMEWORK FOR JUST IMMIGRATION REFORM

A viable framework for just immigration reform must address three areas of general concern. These general areas are divided up temporally—past, present, and future—but should come together in the framework I propose to form one coherent policy. The first area of general concern is the past and how much weight it should be given in crafting an immigration policy. This is because immigrants, for the most part, do not simply leave their home countries willy-nilly. Some of the reasons for why immigrants leave their home countries were already alluded to in Chapter 5 and I referred to

obligation

them generally as "push" and "pull" factors. These factors have a source and depending on the source certain countries might have more or less obligations to admit certain immigrants.

For example, in her insightful book, *"They Take Our Jobs!" and 20 Other Myths about Immigration*, Aviva Chomsky has argued that mere disparities in resources do not themselves create a need or demand for migration—as some might naturally assume. Migration trends, she argues, are better understood when seen as structured along certain historical relationships, like colonialism. As she writes:

> Colonialism sets up a system in which colonized peoples work for those who colonized them. This system is not erased after direct colonialism ends. Rather, it evolves and develops. The colonizer continues to use former colonial subjects as cheap workers, and the unequal economic relationships is also reinforced in this way. Immigration is just one piece of this larger puzzle, interlocking with all the other pieces.[2]

An account like this shows how certain structures (in this case the relationship between the colonized and colonizer) do not simply come to an end when the formal relationship ends (e.g., when colonies obtain political independence), but can continue in different forms by transforming the prior obvert relationship of political domination to one of covert economic domination.

In other words, immigration (and especially undocumented immigration) cannot be understood without seeing it as part of a historical process—in our particular case an exploitive economic process—that continues into the present. Theorists and activists such as David Bacon have persuasively argued, for example, that the free-trade agreements initiated by (and that have largely benefited) countries like the US are also primary contributors of the push and pull factors that are bringing Latin American immigrants to the US and in greater numbers than current US immigration policy allows.[3]

To put this even more simply, a framework for just immigration reform is impossible without adequately taking into account historical legacies like colonialism and other similar relationships that have solidified the constant exchange of people.[4] To the extent that political communities might have an unconstrained right to exclude immigrants, that right as we have seen is contingent upon them being legitimate. It is not clear how much discretion an illegitimate political community (i.e., a community that has unfairly benefited from exploitive relationships and has not made any sincere efforts at reparations) is entitled to have. The radical approach, as mentioned at the end of Chapter 5 would suggest it has none or at least none with regard to certain parts of the world and I tend to agree.

Beyond performing acts of restitution for past injustices (which should be done irrespective of concerns for immigration policy), political communities must also take into account the push and pull factors that have resulted from past relations that were not necessarily unjust (e.g., large-scale guest-worker programs). This is because all past actions have a certain inertia that is never quickly or easily brought to a halt. Most undocumented immigrants today, I believe, would have lawful status if historical realities were better reflected in current immigration policies.

A second area of general concern is the present. This area of attention focuses on the fate of noncitizen residents, both documented and undocumented. With regard to this area of general concern, it would be necessary to develop a method to normalize the status of undocumented immigrants, clear the backlogs for family reunification—especially immediate family members such as children, parents, and spouses—fix current guest-worker programs and end the practice of "deportable offenses" in criminal law (e.g., crimmigration).

A pathway to normalization is a necessary for any just immigration reform. This is because it is not feasible, and maybe even immoral, to believe that millions of people can simply be rounded up and deported. A process of normalization does not need to be unconditional. It can have various stipulations attached to it (e.g., years of residence, good standing during those years, fines . . . etc.), but a clear and reasonable normalization process is essential. The same reasoning holds with regard to family reunification. To believe that a person will not try to reunite with their immediate family members, even at great costs to themselves, is folly. Furthermore, an effort to keep immediate family members apart seems deeply immoral.[5] This is not to say that there could not be some reasonable limit on family reunifications, but the current wait times in places like the US are unreasonable and create perverse incentives for people to circumvent the law rather than to follow it. In the US, the current minimum wait for sponsoring spouses or minor children could be up to five years, and it is much longer if the son or daughter is already over eighteen years of age. For example, if the son or daughter is from Mexico and over the age of eighteen, the current wait time to get into the US is close to seventeen years![6]

Another issue that must be addressed is the fact that the economies of immigrant-receiving countries depend greatly on the labor of immigrants. Guest-worker programs have historically been used to take advantage of this labor by allowing vulnerable immigrants—vulnerable because they can be deported if they lose their job—to enter the country, work for a certain fixed time, and then return home. Guest-worker programs basically create a second-class workforce, a pool of workers who have little to no leverage in their places of work. This group of workers is, in practice if not by contract, denied certain basic rights under the threat of deportation if they complain. There is also no mechanism in place to motivate or compel employers to pay these workers any more than bare minimum wage in exchange for performing some of the hardest, dirtiest, and nastiest jobs. In short, guest-worker programs, as they currently exist, are designed to take advantage of some of the world's most vulnerable people, while at the same time not having to take responsibility for them.

The minimalist solution would be something like the following. First, there should be an increase in the allotment of work visas and this increase should reflect the reality of how many workers are needed and from where these workers are actually coming from. So, for example, if more immigrants are coming into the US to work from Central America than from Denmark (regardless of whether this is because of proximity, past relationships, or active recruitment by employers), then guest-worker visas should reflect that fact about the world. If the service or agriculture sector needs immigrant workers, then guest-worker visas should reflect this fact as well. Second, changes to these visas should be made such that it is easier for immigrant workers to unionize and enjoy all the same rights that native workers enjoy. Here I have in mind not just working conditions, but also the right to leave an employer for a better job without the fear of deportation. Lastly there should be some mechanisms in place so that employers pay guest workers a fair rate for their labor. In this way, employers will not be allowed to take unfair advantage—a kind of nefarious windfall profit because—of an immigrant's vulnerable status.

These changes would provide more immigrant workers with a normalized status, a livable wage, recognition of basic rights, and recourse in case of unjust practices. Depending on how long these immigrants remain, a pathway to citizenship should also be made available since political participation and representation are vital to democracy. After all, it is wrong to deny community members in good standing the right to have a say in what their government should be like, which policies they favor, and which ones they oppose. Also, if long-term residents are not allowed to vote, it is unlikely that elected lawmakers will ever take their interests or concerns into account.

It is also important to recognize that not all lawfully admitted immigrants want to become citizens and not all noncitizens are undocumented immigrants. In places like the US, there are a significant number of noncitizen legally permanent residents. This group of immigrants does not enjoy many of the rights that citizens do (e.g., voting and in some cases access to welfare benefits), but currently they live with the constant threat of deportation. In the US, any immigrant noncitizen may be deported if he or she commits what are called "deportable offenses." These offenses can include crimes of moral turpitude or aggravated felonies. This raises a serious moral problem. Even assuming that a legitimate state has some right to exclude certain noncitizens, why does it necessarily have the right to deport noncitizens it has previously admitted for permanent residence, especially when those residents have lived in the country for an extended period of time?

The answer should be that it does not. Once a country has admitted a person for permanent residence that country has assumed responsibility for them. While crimes of moral turpitude or aggravated felonies can be very serious and sometimes reprehensible, it is unjust to have people who already paid for their crime (e.g., served time in prison) be deported after the fact. This is too close to being a form of double punishment.

There is also the problem that in deporting people for having broken the law, a country is merely exporting its criminals to another country. The case of Honduras serves as an excellent example. Since the late 1990's the US has deported hundreds of gang members back to Honduras. Most of these deportees were raised and lived almost exclusively in the US before being deported. In essence they honed their criminal craft on the streets of the US and when deported to Honduras they brought those skills with them. They then used those skills to start some of the most violent gangs that Honduras has ever seen. This increase in gang violence, ironically, has in turn led to a refugee crisis in Central America that has brought thousands of unaccompanied minors to the US.[7] A just immigration reform would therefore remove the practice of deportable offenses both because it is unjust to the noncitizen resident and also because it presents an unfair imposition on countries that are forced to take in these deportees.

The third area of general concern is the future. If the ultimate goal is to bring unauthorized immigration to an end and also to help immigrants who are admitted better acclimate to and feel as though they are part of their new communities, then the roots of displacement and xenophobia must be addressed. To address this last area, I argue that there is going to have to be a concerted effort by international entities like the IMF and the World Bank to both forgive the debt of poor countries and end structural adjustment programs (and any other variants of these sorts of programs), which in many cases have been part of the original loan agreements that have resulted in the loss of social safety nets in immigrant-sending countries. In places where these economic programs have failed, sustainable economic plans need to be put in place that will help many of these countries build up their own economies. These sorts of actions are also more consistent with the original mandate of institutions like the IMF and World Bank then the neo-liberal agenda they have followed for the last few decades.

The way to end economic displacement, which more accurately describes the condition of most undocumented immigrants today, is to create an environment in which people do not need to leave their home countries in order to have a minimally decent life. Creating this sort of environment requires that the international community be proactive, rather than reactive, in helping to curb future mass migration. In short all people should, as the title of one of David Bacon's books suggests, have the right to stay home.[8]

Lastly, immigrant-receiving countries need to develop realistic admission and exclusion policies. Even when admission and exclusion policies appear "fair," if they are only enforceabled through unjust means, then they raise the specter of potentially ostracizing certain residents, including citizens, as perpetual foreigners. Social trust therefore depends less on stricter enforcement, and more on having an immigration policy that is reflective of socio-historical circumstances and is flexible enough to account for future changes in those circumstances. For example, it is a fact that the US economy will continue to draw in immigrants from certain parts of the world more than it will from other parts. This is either because of its historical or geographical connections to those areas of the world or for other reasons. A successful immigration policy should reflect that, but at the same time should be flexible enough to adjust if and when conditions change.

A just immigration reform should be able to address all three areas of general concern. These areas of concern have been presented here as separate, but as we have already started to see they cannot be adequately addressed in isolation from one another. A just immigration reform will have to take into account the past, while looking toward the future as it crafts its immigration policy for the present. Lastly, while this account is in many ways consistent with an open-borders position, it does not necessarily entail that borders be completely open. It does, however, entail a circumvention of the types of immigration policies a political community may justly adopt.

CONCLUSION

The framework outlined in this chapter appears to take what many would consider a radical stance on most of the controversial questions surrounding immigration. For example, this framework rejects enforcement strategies such as "prevention through deterrence" and "attrition through enforcement." It suggests that past injustices, such as colonialism, must be taken into consideration when developing an immigration policy. It provides a case for giving amnesty to undocumented immigrants, expanding guest-worker programs in a way that both protects immigrants and better reflects economic realities. It also argues that legal permanent residents should not be subject to deportation, even when they have committed serious criminal offenses. Lastly, it argues that reforms should aim to make future immigration less a matter of necessity and more of an option for people.

As I have tried to show, these stances are not really all that radical and in fact are more consistent with the central tenants of a constitutional democracy. These stances appear radical only because the immigration policies of most countries are currently stuck in a *security dilemma*. This dilemma blinds us to the possibilities that could be afforded if we prioritize the liberty concern over the security concern, as most liberal moral and political philosophers have done. The difference between my account and that of other most liberal moral and political philosophers is that I take the issue of enforcement to be central to the question of immigration justice. Most liberal moral and political philosophers have not and therefore gloss over one of the more important aspects of the immigration debate.

The minimalist account I have put forward in this book gets us out of the *liberty dilemma* by prioritizing immigrant rights. This account is not only the most philosophically consistent, but as I hoped to have shown in the prior section, it is also the one with the most feasible public policy implications. The three-part framework for immigration reform provided above takes into account the issue of immigration in its entirety, from policies of admission and exclusion to practices of enforcement. But while taking enforcement into account, this framework also has not gotten stuck on enforcement, as "enforcement first" models of immigration reform tend to do. This framework gets beyond enforcement and also looks to address the root causes (and not just the symptoms) of the current "immigration problem." Lastly, while this book has been primarily focused on contemporary US immigration, its insights are hopefully general enough that they can also be applicable to other circumstances and contexts.

NOTES

1. For an argument that puts Wellman in a similar bind, but for different reasons see Javier Hidalgo & Christopher Freiman, "Liberalism or Immigration Restrictions, But Not Both," *Journal of Ethics and Social Philosophy* 10.2 (2016).

2. Aviva Chomsky, *"They Take Our Jobs!" and 20 Other Myths about Immigration* (Boston, MA: Beacon Press Books, 2007), 146.

3. See David Bacon, *The Right to Stay Home: How US Policy Drives Mexican Migration* (Boston, MA: Beacon Press Boston, 2013).

4. Thomas Nail has recently suggested that we take this kind of historical view even further, arguing that we should see "the migrant" as the exemplar of the new political subject and that by doing so we would have to rethink our current static political ontologies toward an ontology based more on "movement." This is a fascinating approach to migration theory and political philosophy in general, but one that is beyond the scope of this book. See Thomas Nail. *The Figure of the Migrant* (Stanford: Stanford University Press, 2015).

5. For an excellent philosophical defense of making family reunification a priority in immigration policy see Matthew Lister, "Immigration, Association, and the Family," *Law and Philosophy* 29.6 (2010): 717–745.

6. Daniel Huang, "A Devastating Wait: Family Unity and the Immigration Backlogs," (United States: Asian Pacific American Legal Center, 2008), 10.

7. Michael Daly, "The Deported L.A. Gangs Behind This Border Kid Crisis," *The Daily Beast*, July 11, 2014, Accessed August 21, 2015, http://www.thedailybeast.com/articles/2014/07/11/the-deported-l-a-gangs-behind-this-border-kid-crisis.html

8. Bacon, *The Right to Stay Home*, 2013.

Bibliography

1943 Magnuson Act, H.R. 3070; Pub.L. 78–199; 57 Stat. 600. 78th Congress; December 17, 1943.

1965 Immigration and Nationality Act, H.R. 2580; Pub.L. 89–236; 79 Stat. 911. 89th Congress., 2nd sess., (October 3, 1965).

Arash Abizadeh, "Democratic Theory and Border Coercion: No Right to Unilaterally Control Your Own Borders," *Political Theory* 36.1 (2008): 37–65.

———. "Democratic Legitimacy and State Coercion: A Reply to David Miller," *Political Theory* 38.1 (2010): 121–130.

Afroyim v. Rusk. 387 U.S. 253, 1967.

Agamben, Giorgio. *Homo Sacer: Sovereign Power and Bare Life.* Trans. Daniel Heller-Roazen. Stanford: Stanford University Press, 1998.

———. *Remnants of Auschwitz: The Witness and the Archive.* Trans. Daniel Heller-Roazen. New York: Zone Books, 1999.

———. *State of Exception.* Trans. Kevin Attell. Chicago: The University of Chicago Press, 2005.

Arendt, Hannah. *The Origins of Totalitarianism.* New York: Shocken Books, 2004.

Arizona v. United States, 567 U.S. 2012.

Bacon, David. *The Children of NAFTA: Labor Wars on the U.S./Mexico Border.* Berkeley and Los Angles, California: University of California Press, 1997.

———. *Illegal People: How Globalization Creates Migration and Criminalizes Immigrants.* Boston, Massachusetts: Beacon Press, 2008.

———. *The Right to Stay Home: How US Policy Drives Mexican Migration* Boston, MA: Beacon Press Boston, 2013.

Bader, Veit. "Citizenship and Exclusion. Radical Democracy, Community, and Justice. Or, What Is Wrong with Communitarianism?" *Political Theory* 23. 2 (1995): 211–246.

Beitz, Charles R. "Justice and International Relations." *Philosophy & Public Affairs* 4.4 (1975): 360–389.

Benhabib, Seyla. *The Rights of Others: Aliens, Residents, and Citizens.* Cambridge, UK: Cambridge, 2004.

Bentham, Jeremy. "Anarchical Fallacies; Being an Examination of the Declarations of Rights Issued During the French Revolution—an Examination of the Rights of Man and the Citizen Decreed by the Constituent Assembly in France." *The Works of Jeremy Bentham Vol 2.* Ed. John Bowring. London: Elibron Classics, 2005.

Berlin, Isaiah. "Two Concepts of Liberty." *Four Essays on Liberty.* London: Oxford University Press, 1958.

Blake, Michael. "Immigration." In *A Companion To Applied Ethics.* Ed. R.G. Frey and Christopher Heath Wellman. Oxford: Blackwell Publishing, 2003.

———. "Immigration, Association, and Antidiscrimination," *Ethics* 122.4 (2012): 748–762.

———. "Immigration, Jurisdiction, and Exclusion," *Philosophy and Public Affairs* 41.2 (2013): 103–130.

Bodin, Jean. *Six Books of the Commonwealth.* Trans. M.J. Tooley. Oxford: Blackwell, 1955.

Boettcher, James W. "Immigration Policy and Civic-Political Identity," *Public Affairs Quarterly,* 27.1 (2013): 1–23.

Brian, Tara and Frank Laczko Ed., "Fatal Journeys: Tracking Lives Lost during Migration," *International Organization for Migration,* 1.1 (2014).

Brimelow, Peter. *Alien Nation: Common Sense About America's Immigration Disaster.* New York: Harper Perennial, 1996.

Brown v. Board of Education of Topeka. 347 U.S. 483, 1954.

"Budget-in-Brief Fiscal-Year 2016," *Department of Homeland Security.* Accessed November 19, 2015. http://www.dhs.gov/sites/default/files/publications/FY_2016_DHS_Budget_in_Brief.

Burke, Edmond. *Reflections on the Revolution in France.* London: Penguin Books, 2004.

Carens, Joseph H. "Aliens and Citizens: The case for Open Borders," *The Rights of Minority Cultures.* Oxford: Oxford University Press, 1997.

———. "The Rights of Irregular Migrants," *Ethics & International Affairs* 22.2 (2008): 163–186.

Cavallero, Eric. "Association and Asylum," *Philosophical Studies,* 169.1 (2014): 133–141.

Chae Chan Ping v. United States. 130 U.S. 581, 1889.

Chacon, Justin Akers and Mike Davis. *No One Is Illegal: Fighting Racism and State Violence on the U.S.- Mexico Border.* Chicago: Haymarket Books, 2006.

Chomsky, Aviva. *"They Take Our Jobs!" and 20 Other Myths About Immigration.* Massachusetts: Beacon Press books, 2007.

"Chinese Exclusion Act of 1882." Ch.126, 47th cong., 1st Sess., 1882.

Cole, Phillip. *Philosophies of Exclusion: Liberal Political Theory and Immigration.* Edinburgh, Great Britain: Edinburgh University Press, 2000.

Cornelius, Wayne A. "Controling 'Unwanted' Immigration: Lessons From the United States, 1993–2004," *Journal of Ethnic and Migration Studies* 31.4 (2005): 775–794.

Coulter, Ann. *Adios, America: The Left's Plan to Turn Our Country into a Third World Hellhole.* Washington, DC: Regnery Publishing, 2015.

Daly, Michael. "The Deported L.A. Gangs Behind This Border Kid Crisis," *The Daily Beast,* July 11, 2014, accessed August 21, 2015, http://www.thedailybeast.com/articles/2014/07/11/the-deported-l-a-gangs-behind-this-border-kid-crisis.html

Deudney, Daniel. "Binding Sovereigns: Authorities, Structures, and Geopolitics in Philadelphian Systems." *State Sovereignty as Social Construct,* edited by Thomas Biersteker and Cynthia Weber, 190–238. Melbourne, Australia: Cambridge University Press, 1996.

Diaz, Kim. "U.S. Border Wall: A Poggean Analysis of Illegal Immigration." *Philosophy in the Contemporary World* 17.1 (2010): 1–12.

Feere, Jon. "Reining in Zadvydas v. Davis: New Bill Aimed at Stopping Release of Criminal Aliens." *Center for Immigration Studies* May 2011. Accessed August 15, 2014. http://www.cis.org/stopping-release-of-criminal-aliens

Ferracioli, Luara. "Family Migration Schemes and Liberal Neutrality: A Dilemma," *Journal of Moral Philosophy* 13.5 (2016): 553–575.

Fine, Sarah. "Freedom of Association Is Not the Answer." *Ethics* 120 (2010): 338–356.

Fong Yue Ting v. United States. 149 U.S. 698, 1893. "French Senate votes to ban Islamic full veil in public." *BBC News.* September 14 2010, accessed January 20, 2012, http://www.bbc.co.uk/news/world-europe-11305033

Freiman, Christopher and Javier Hidalgo "Liberalism or Immigration Restrictions, But Not Both," *Journal of Ethics and Social Philosophy* 10.2 (2016): 1–22.

Guidi, Ruxandra. "Honduran LA Resident Accidentally Deported, then Dies in Prison Fire" *Southern California Public Radio* March 2, 2012, accessed May 10, 2012, http://www.scpr.org/news/2012/03/02/31481/honduran-resident-los-angeles-wrongfully-deported.

Higgins, Peter. *Immigration Justice.* Edinburgh: Edinburgh University Press, 2013.

Hobbes, Thomas. *Leviathan.* Ed. Edwin Curley. Indianapolis: Hackett Publishing, 1994.

Huang, Daniel. "A Devastating Wait: Family Unity and the Immigration Backlogs." *Asian Pacific American Legal Center* 2008, accessed May 10, 2014, http://www.advancingjustice-aajc.org/sites/aajc/files/APALC_family_report.pdf

Hume, David. "Of the Original Contract." *Political Writings.* Ed. Stuart D. Warner and Donald W. Livingston, 164–181. Indianapolis: Hackett Publishing, 1994.

———. "Of Parties in General." *Political Writings.* Ed. Stuart D. Warner and Donald W. Livingston, 157–164. Indianapolis: Hackett Publishing Company, 1994.

———. "Of the Origin of Justice and Property." *Political Writings.* Ed. Stuart D. Warner and Donald W. Livingston, 7–20. Indianapolis: Hackett Publishing Company, 1994.

———. *An Enquiry Concerning The Principles of Morals.* Ed. J.B. Schneewind. Indianapolis: Hackett Publishing Company, 1983.

Huemer, Michael. "Is There a Right to Immigrate." *Social Theory and Practice* 36.3 (2010): 429–461.

Huntington, Samuel. *Who Are We? The Challenges to America's National Identity.* New York: Simon & Schuster Paperbacks, 2004.

"Immigration Enforcement Within the United States," Congressional Research Service, *The Library of Congress*, April 6, 2006, Accessed December 21, 2014, http://www.fas.org/sgp/crs/misc/RL33351.pdf.

"Immigration and Naturalization Service," *Department of Justice* Accessed November 19, 2015. http://www.justice.gov/archive/jmd/1975_2002/2002/html/page104–108.htm

Johnson, Kevin R. *The "Huddled Masses" Myth: Immigration and Civil Rights.* Philadelphia: Temple University Press, 2004.

Kant, Immanuel. "On the Proverb: That May be True in Theory, But Is of No Practical Use." *Perpetual Peace and Other Essays.* Trans. Ted Humphrey. Indianapolis/ Cambridge: Hackett Publishing Company, 1983.

———. "Grounding For The Metaphysics Of Morals." *Ethical Philosophy.* Trans. James Ellington. Indianapolis: Hackett Publishing Company, 1983.

———. "An Answer to the Question: What is Enlightenment?," *Perpetual Peace and Other Essays.* Trans. Ted Humphrey. Indianapolis/ Cambridge: Hackett Publishing Company, 1983.

Krikorian, Mark. "Attrition Through Enforcement Will Work," *San Diego Union Tribune*, April 2, 2006, accessed May 23, 2015, http://www.utsandiego.com/union-trib/20060402/news_mz1e02krikor.html.

Lister, Matthew. "Immigration, Association, and the Family," *Law and Philosophy* 29.6 (2010): 717–745.

Locke, John. *Second Treaties of Government.* Ed. C.B. Macpherson. Indianapolis: Hackett Publishing, 1980.

Roberto Lovato, "Juan Crow in Georgia" *The Nation*, May 26, 2008. http://www.thenation.com/article/juan-crow-georgia. Accessed December 21, 2014.

Machiavelli, Niccolo. "The Prince." *The Prince and the Discourses.* Trans. Luigi Ricci. New York: Random House,1950.

———. "Discourses on the First Ten Books of Titus Livius."*The Prince and the Discourses.* Trans. Christian E. Detmold. New York: Modern Library, 1950.

Marx, Karl and Frederick Engels. *The Communist Manifesto.* Trans. Samuel Moore. Ed. David McLellan. Oxford/New York: Oxford University Press, 1998.

———.*Capital Vol 3: A Critique of Political Economy.* Trans. David Fernbach. London: Penguin Classics, 1991.

Mendieta, Eduardo. "The Right to Political Membership: Democratic Morality and the Right of Irregular Immigrants." *Radical Philosophy Review* 14.2 (2011): 177–185.

Mill, John Stuart. *Utilitarianism.* Ed. George Sher. Indianapolis: Hackett Publishing Company, 2001.

———. *On Liberty.* Ed. Elizabeth Rapaport. Indianapolis: Hackett Publishing Company, 1978.

Mills, Charles. "The Domination Contract." In *Contract and Domination*, Carole Pateman and Charles Mills, 79–105. Malden, MA: Polity Press, 2007.

Miller, David. "Immigration: The Case for Limits." In *Contemporary Debates in Applied Ethics.* Ed. Andrew I. Cohen, and Christopher Heath Wellman, 193–206. Malden MA: Blackwell Publishing, 2005.

———. "Immigrants, Nations, and Citizenship." *The Journal of Political Philosophy* 16. 4 (2008): 371–390.

———. "Why Immigration Controls Are Not Coercive: A Reply to Arash Abizadeh," *Political Theory* 38.1 (2010): 111–120.

Nail, Thomas. *The Figure of the Migrant.* Stanford: Stanford University Press, 2015.

Ngai, Mae. *Impossible Subjects: Illegal Aliens and the Making of Modern America.* Princeton, NJ: Princeton University Press, 2004.

Nozick, Robert. *Anarchy, State and Utopia.* New York: Basic Books, 1974.

Pevnick, Ryan. "Social Trust and the Ethics of Immigration Policy." *The Journal of Political Philosophy* 17. 2 (2009): 146–167.

———. *Immigration and the Constraints of Justice: Between Open Borders and Absolute Sovereignty.* Cambridge: Cambridge University Press, 2011.

Plato. "The Republic." *Plato: Complete Works.* Ed. John M. Cooper. Trans. G.M.A. Grube. Indianapolis: Hackett Publishing Company, 1997: 971–1223.

Plessy v. Ferguson. 163 U.S. 537, 1896.

Plyler v. Doe. 457 U.S. 202, 1982.

Pogge, Thomas W. "Cosmopolitanism and Sovereignty." *Ethics* 103.1 (1992): 48–75.

Powers, Kemp. "Group says U.S. citizen wrongly deported to Mexico" *Reuters* June 11, 2007, accessed May 10, 2012, http://www.reuters.com/article/2007/06/11/us-usa-immigration-deportation-idUSN1118919320070611.

Rawls, John. *A Theory of Justice.* Cambridge, Massachusetts: Harvard University Press, 1971.

———. *Justice As Fairness: A Restatement.* Ed. Erin Kelly. Cambridge, Massachusetts: Harvard University Press, 2001.

———. *The Law Of Peoples.* Cambridge, Massachusetts: Harvard University Press, 1999.

———. *Political Liberalism.* New York: Columbia University Press, 2005.

Reed-Sandoval, Amy. "Oaxacan Transborder Communities and the Political Philosophy of Immigration." *International Journal of Applied Philosophy* 30.1 (2016): 91–104.

Robbins, Ted. "Nearly Half of Illegal Immigrants Overstay Visas," *NPR*, June 14, 2006, accessed September 15, 2011, http://www.npr.org/templates/story/story.php?storyId=5485917.

Rousseau, Jean-Jacques. "On the Social Contract." *The Basic Political Writings.* Trans. Donald Cress. Indianapolis: Hackett Publishing, 1987.

———. "Discourse on the Origin of Inequality." *The Basic Political Writings.* Trans. Donald Cress. Indianapolis: Hackett Publishing, 1987.

Sánchez, Carlos Alberto. "On Documents and Subjectivity," *Radical Philosophy Review* 14.2 (2011): 197–205

———. "Philosophy and the Post-Immigrant Fear," *Philosophy in the Contemporary World* 18.1 (2011): 31–42.

Schmitt, Carl. *Political Theology.* Chicago: The University of Chicago Press, 1985.

Sidgwick, Henry. *The Methods of Ethics.* Chicago: University of Chicago Press, 1962.

Silva, Grant J. "On the Militarization of Borders and the Juridical Right to Exclude," *Public Affairs Quarterly* 29.2 (2015): 217–234.

Silverman, Stephanie J. "Detaining Immigrants and Asylum Seekers: A Normative Introduction" *Critical Review of International Social and Political Philosophy* 17.5 (2014): 600–617.

Smith v. Turner; Norris v. Boston. 48 U.S. 283, 1849.

State of Arizona Senate, Forty-Ninth Legislature, Second Regular Session 2010, Senate Bill 1070

Trop v. Dulles. 356 U.S. 86, 70, 1958.

U.S. Constitution. "Unauthorized Immigrant Population Trends for States, Birth Countries and Regions," *Pew Research Center,* Dec. 11, 2014. Accessed November 19, 2015. http://www.pewhispanic.org/2014/12/11/unauthorized-trends/#All

Velásquez, Ernesto Rosen. "States of Violence and the Right to Exclude" *Journal of Poverty*, DOI: 10.1080/10875549.2016.1186777: 1–21

Vaughan, Jessica. "Attrition Through Enforcement: A Cost-Effective Strategy to Shrink the Illegal Population," *Center for Immigration Studies*, April 2006, accessed September 15, 2011, http://www.cis.org/Enforcement-IllegalPopulation.

Von Hayek, Friedrich. *The Constitution of Liberty.* Chicago: University of Chicago Press, 1960.

Walzer, Michael. *Spheres of Justice: A Defense of Pluralism and Equality.* New York: Basic Books, 1983.

———. "Response to Veit Bader," *Political Theory* 23.2 (1995): 247–248.

Wellman, Christopher Heath. "Immigration and Freedom of Association." *Ethics* 119 (2008): 109–141.

———. "Immigration Restrictions in the Real World," *Philosophical Studies* 169.1 (2014): 119–122.

Wellman, Christopher Heath and Phillip Cole. *Debating the Ethics of Immigration: Is There a Right to Exclude.* New York: Oxford University Press, 2011.

Wilcox, Shelley. "Immigrant Admissions and Global Relations of Harm." *Journal of Social Philosophy* 38. (2007): 274–279.

———. "Culture, National Identity, and Admission to Citizenship." *Social Theory and Practice*, 30.4 (2004): 559–583.

Williams, Reginald. "Illegal Immigration: A Case for Residency." *Public Affairs Quarterly* 23.4 (2009): 309–324.

Wong Wing v. United States. 163 U.S. 228, 1896.

Zadvydas v. Davis. 533 U.S. 678, 2001.

Index

About the Author

José Jorge Mendoza is an assistant professor of philosophy at the University of Massachusetts Lowell and is co-editor of *Radical Philosophy Review*. His areas of specialization are in moral and political philosophy, philosophy of race, and Latin American philosophy. His current research is on global justice and in particular on the tension between democratic autonomy (i.e., a peoples' right to self-determination) and universal human rights.

About the Author